Next Steps in Teaching

This book charts the first steps in your early teaching career: from finishing your teacher training programme, through your probationary year, and into the comparatively settled routine of your second and third years in teaching. It provides a longer term perspective on teaching which will help put present challenges into proportion. The book aims to:

- Help you orient yourself through the pitfalls of teaching
- Describe some of the challenges and difficulties you might face in the classroom and provide advice based on the experiences of other teachers
- Describe the successful strategies new teachers have used to develop their teaching
- Highlight the satisfaction of teaching

The book contains interviews with new teachers and short case studies. These will help to show the journeys that other new teachers have taken and how they came out as confident and fluent teachers. The opportunity to hear these stories might help you see your own discomforts as small but important steps along the way and your own successes as part of a wider picture.

Michael Hammond is a senior lecturer in education at the University of Warwick where he coordinates a PGCE course.

Next Steps in Teaching

A guide to starting your career in
the secondary school

Michael Hammond

Routledge
Taylor & Francis Group

LONDON AND NEW YORK

First published 2005 by Routledge
2 Park Square, Milton Park, Abingdon, Oxon OX14 4RN

Simultaneously published in the USA and Canada
by Routledge
270 Madison Ave, New York, NY 10016

Routledge is an imprint of the Taylor & Francis Group

© 2005 Michael Hammond

Typeset in Galliard by
Florence Production Ltd, Stoodleigh, Devon
Printed and bound in Great Britain by
TJ International Ltd, Padstow, Cornwall

British Library Cataloguing in Publication Data
A catalogue record for this book is available from the British Library

Library of Congress Cataloging in Publication Data
A catalog record for this book has been requested

ISBN 0-415-31734-7

Contents

Appendices   175

Illustrations

Figures

Boxes

Acknowledgements

This book arose from research carried out with student teachers at the University of Warwick which explored their experiences of training to teach and went on to track their development as teachers over their first four years in school. I am indebted to the teachers who have taken part in this research for their patience and openness in discussing their experiences of teaching. I would also like to thank Victoria Cartwright, Diane Levine and Shazia Mumtaz for their support and insight in helping carry out the research.

To put the experiences of these teachers in a larger context, focus group meetings were carried out with teachers of a wide range of subjects who were in the early stages of their careers. Again, I am grateful to teachers who took part in this research and to Barbara Shaw for the work she carried out. Both projects were supported by the University of Warwick Teaching and Learning Development Fund, for which I am grateful.

I would like to acknowledge the insight I was offered into early professional development by working with my colleagues Janet Ainley, Ann Barnes, Liz Bills, Val Brooks, Marilyn Hunt, Yvette Kingston, Alison Kitson and Kate Shilvock in developing a programme to support new teachers, and to thank Peter Lang for answering my query concerning pastoral education. In addition, I benefited from working with Mayuresh Shah in developing support materials for pupil tracking. I would like to thank Ian Abbott, Ann Barnes, Jo Crozier, Penny Nunn and Abeer Abdel Salam for reading and commenting on an earlier version of the text and Neelum Deu and Sarah Noble for reading particular chapters. Finally, I would like to thank Ana, Gareth, Jo, Moira and Rosie for being ever willing to give me the learner's perspective on teaching.

Introduction
Who is this book for?

This book is aimed in the first instance at student teachers in secondary schools who are about to complete their period of training and looking ahead to their first years in teaching. However, it will also interest newly qualified teachers and those responsible for mentoring and supporting student and newly qualified teachers. The book aims to:

- help orient you through your first years of teaching;
- highlight the satisfaction of teaching;
- describe successful strategies new teachers have taken to develop their teaching;
- review some of the challenges and difficulties you might face in the classroom and provide advice to meet those challenges;
- provide signposts to relevant resources;
- help you reflect on your career and plan your professional development.

Your first years of teaching are particularly important in establishing your career and it is hoped that this book will help you make the most of the opportunities open to you.

The structure of the book follows a time line. Part I asks you to take stock as you near the end of your training programme. Chapter 1 looks at how your training programme has affected your motivation, your understanding of teaching and the values that you try to express in your teaching. In Chapter 2 you are asked to consider your strengths in planning, subject knowledge, classroom teaching and assessment and how identifying these strengths can boost your self-confidence. You are then asked to identify your areas for development and consider recently expressed concerns in the teaching of pupils from ethnic minorities and pupils with English as an additional language

(EAL); the use of ICT; and assessment of pupils. Chapter 3 covers the various strategies available to develop your teaching during your training programme. The key to your development lies in under-standing and adapting to the demands made on you in the classroom, but as your training programme finishes you are encouraged to get a wider view of teaching by further observation of other teachers and visits to other schools.

Part II considers your first two years in school. Chapter 4 looks at preparing for your first term as a newly qualified teacher. It discusses what you bring to the school, and what you can do to prepare for your classes. It highlights the satisfaction to be gained from teaching and the energy and enthusiasm you might feel at the start of your career, before looking at some of the difficulties you might encounter and strategies for dealing with those difficulties. Some new teachers talk of being overwhelmed in their first year: strategies to manage your time and commitment are examined.

Chapter 5 looks at progression in your teaching and the different patterns of support that schools offer new teachers. The role of the career entry and professional development (CEPD) profile is discussed along with the role of the induction standards for new teachers. Chapter 6 looks further ahead to your second year of teaching. You now have much more knowledge and experience on which to draw and the implications of this are examined with respect to preparation for the new term, further development of your teaching and facing up to continuing challenges within the classroom. This chapter also looks at new roles and responsibilities in your department.

Part III is a single chapter which looks back at key messages about learning to teach and looks ahead to the development of your career in the longer term. You are best served by a school that provides you with a community of practice. Many schools fall short of this ideal and the pros and cons of moving school are considered. Support for continuing professional development (CPD) in its widest sense is next described enabling you to be proactive in developing your career. Finally, the chapter looks at concerns over career rewards, workloads and career progression through teacher threshold payments and advanced skills status. The enduring appeal of teaching is discussed.

A key feature of the book is that it looks at teaching from the perspective of the new teacher. It considers how you can be proactive in identifying, and positive in taking advantage of, opportunities to develop your teaching and your career. However, not everything is in your control. Experiences of training and induction programmes differ greatly, as do ways in which schools cater for long-term career development. The chapters draw on the experiences of student teachers and new teachers, and on wider research literature, to illustrate the opportunities and constraints when taking your next steps in teaching. Each chapter is interspersed with focus questions and activities. The focus questions invite you to pause in order to consider the implications that a description, a scenario or a case study might have for you, and for your teaching. The activities invite you to carry out a review, to collect examples of work, to meet with a colleague or induction tutor, to plan an observation of a lesson, to observe a lesson, to carry out an innovation and so on. The focus questions and activities are nearly always related to, and help support you through, a training or induction programme or CPD in its widest sense.

Another important feature of the book is that it takes a longer term view of learning to teach. As teachers, we are often understandably focused on the short term: what are we going to teach this class next week or next lesson or even right now? A longer perspective puts present challenges into proportion. Others have gone through similar journeys and have come out confident and fluent teachers. The opportunity to hear their stories might help you see the challenges you face as small but important steps on the way.

While learning to teach you will have experienced mood swings, changes in your teaching style and highs and lows in your relations with the youngsters you teach. Expect this to continue. However, a recurring constant for you, and for the teachers whose work is discussed in this book, is the importance of the relationship with the children you teach. This relationship is described as a major motivation for going into teaching and a major source of satisfaction in the classroom.

Teaching has had a mixed press in the last few years. Government agencies have been keen to tell us that 'no one forgets a good teacher'. We now have annual awards for teachers and the latest examination successes of pupils and schools are trumpeted on television and in the papers. New teachers have been praised as 'the best trained that we have ever had' (OFSTED 2003). The diversification of schools has rightly been the matter of debate and argument but undoubtedly many teachers are enjoying more varied and more flexible career options than in the past. Many teachers continue to enjoy the job of teaching and feel a high level of satisfaction.

Set against this positive view of teaching has been an unrelenting barrage of initiatives and change, at times oppressive inspection regimes and disruptive behaviour in the classroom. There are widespread teacher shortages caused by difficulties in recruitment but, more importantly, in retention. Many new teachers begin their career with high hopes and enthusiasm only to become disappointed by the overly bureaucratic nature of the job and, in some cases, lack of support from parents (Smithers and Robinson 2003; Adams 2003). Everyone is conscious of the uneven conditions and standards within schools.

Are you entering a system in crisis or a golden age of teaching? You will need to keep an open mind but there are undoubtedly opportunities for you to make a difference. I hope this book will help you do so.

For readers outside England

The book is based, for the most part, on working and talking with teachers in England but the picture it paints will be familiar to many readers in other parts of the UK and, indeed, much further afield. At times, particular aspects of starting a teaching career in England are described, for example the induction arrangements, the salaries, the support for continuing professional development. Many of these apply in the same way to teachers in Wales. However, there are occasional variations and a potential for greater diversity in the years ahead which makes it more accurate, and more appropriate, to talk about the situation in England rather than England and Wales. These arrangements often raise issues that are relevant to teachers in other countries and it might be useful to provide some further background for readers who are unfamiliar with programmes of teaching training in England. Teacher training in England is managed, on behalf of the Department for Education and Science (DfES), by the Teacher Training Agency (TTA). The most common route into teaching in England, and indeed the UK as a whole, is a one-year full-time postgraduate certificate in education (PGCE) course based at a higher education institution. These courses are run in partnerships with local schools: student teachers spend at least 24 weeks of an academic year in a school or, more likely, two schools. Some providers offer a two-year course giving more time to develop subject knowledge. It is still commonly assumed that most people enter a PGCE course immediately on graduating, but the age profile is varied and around half of student teachers are aged 25 or over. There are also some flexible PGCE course routes designed to meet individual needs and circumstances, for example, to fit training over a number of years around a full-time job. Other options for

training are School Centred Initial Teacher Training (SCITT) programmes. These training programmes are run by schools, sometimes
with input from higher education institutions and local education
authorities (LEAs). Meanwhile, the Graduate and Registered Teacher
Programme (GRTP) enables schools to employ people who are not yet
qualified to teach and train them through an individual training programme. There is also a Fast Track programme designed to develop
those with 'the highest potential for excellence in teaching'. This is an
optional additional route within several programmes but one for which
certain criteria need to be met. All student teachers are eligible for a
£6,000 training bursary. For more information about training routes,
turn to the Teacher Training Agency web site, and for information on
any of the organisations or key terms mentioned in the book go to the
appendices at the back of the book. These contain web addresses (urls)
where appropriate.

Part 1

As you near the final stages of your training programme

Chapter 1

Your personal commitment to teaching

Before taking your next steps in teaching you might find it helpful to look back at what led you into teaching, your special contribution to teaching and how you are going to sustain your commitment in the future. This first chapter will help you:

- reflect on your motivation to teach;
- identify how your understanding of teaching has changed;
- consider the importance of personal values in teaching.

You and your motivation to teach

Your motivation to teach led you into a training programme and has seen you through a challenging programme of training. Where does this motivation come from? According to most of the literature (for example, Kyriacou *et al.* 1999; Lortie 1975; Reid and Caudwell 1997; Spear *et al.* 2000), the answer will probably lie in a mix. Significant attractions of teaching are its interpersonal nature; the nurturing of young people and making a contribution to society; the involvement with a subject; the career rewards and conditions of work.

To describe teaching as inter-personal is simply saying that it involves working with people. However, teaching involves a special type of relationship with others, one in which you are in a legally recognised position of authority and one that involves you in handing over skills, knowledge and attitudes to young learners. You will have found you need to be comfortable with authority and interested, and better still fascinated, in how to manage the relationship between teachers and taught. Graham, a student teacher, said:

> I wanted to go into teaching as I wanted to see someone, to help someone, be able to achieve in my subject. This gives you a really

big buzz especially when someone thinks they are useless and you get them to do some good work and they actually realise they are not useless. That for me is why I went into it. It is not exactly as I thought it would be. It has been really hard sometimes but I do get the buzz to keep me going.

The buzz to which Graham refers arises from seeing someone do something with his guidance which they could not do previously. This is fundamental to your job satisfaction. You may take pride and confidence in the development of your own skills, but you are also altruistic, teaching is about helping another person. Many go into teaching because they want to contribute to the nurturing of young people and help them to take a full part in society. Several, such as Margaret below, talked about their desire to put something back:

> There were several reasons to decide to teach but one was that I was in close contact with a youngster who was having difficulty in her life and I could see the impact of teaching and the school on her. I'm a great believer that life is about giving something that you have to others, about passing on something you have and I thought that teaching would be the most effective way of doing that, of making a difference.

As teachers, we want to feel we are making a difference and this explains why positive feedback from pupils is so valued. Jonathan had found particular encouragement from the response of challenging pupils – ones he felt he could see with a fresh pair of eyes:

> There was one kid in the class. He had never as far I could see done anything over the year and I was really chuffed because I sat down with him after the lesson, explained what we had been doing to him and why it was important. He responded really well next lesson. He never let on, of course, but his mate said 'He likes you' and that made me feel I had cracked it as a teacher.

Julie was similarly pleased to get an acknowledgement from her class when she was leaving:

> Let me show you this card they did for me. It really made me cry as it had not been easy and they all said how much they had learnt and wished me good luck next year.

In a similar vein, Michael appreciated the feedback at parents' evening:

> It was a great moment when I sat with my mentor at parents' evening. I explained what I was teaching the class and one of the parents said, 'Oh yes my son was talking about you and saying he was enjoying the lessons.' She probably had no idea what it meant to me, but I cannot tell you how important it was.

A further source of motivation is your interest in your subject. You will almost certainly have studied a subject in a great deal of depth and teaching gives you an opportunity to keep up with latest ideas and theories. In Roger's case taking a PGCE course enabled him to keep alive his interest in mathematics:

> I have always been interested in maths and that was a reason to go into teaching. Everything relies on number in some way or most of it. Going into teaching will make me keep up with different aspects of the subject. It is varied and there are new things for me to learn all the time.

It might seem that as a mathematics graduate Roger would have many alternative career opportunities in which to develop his interest in his subject. However, he had found the commercial work he had done on placement too specialist and he missed the variety that had attracted him to doing mathematics in the first place.

There are undoubtedly better paid jobs for graduates than teaching – another mathematics graduate to whom we spoke explained that he was offered far more as a trainee manager at McDonalds than teaching – but it does offer a career structure that is attractive to some people. You will be aware that teaching is not a route to a fortune and many teachers are understandably disgruntled about job rewards, particularly in areas in which the cost of living (in particular the cost of housing) is high. However, there is a structure and an opportunity for advancement that you might find reasonably attractive, particularly if you are entering teaching in mid-career after experiencing poor prospects in other jobs, or redundancy. Of course, the holidays are an attraction of the job though most teachers spend some time at least working during the holidays and work long hours the rest of the year. But, if nothing else, the flexibility to organise your own work in the school holidays is an attraction, particularly if you have your own children.

You will probably have a mix of motivations to teach. For example, you are not likely to be overwhelmed by the material rewards on offer, but they are a factor in reaching a decision to teach. Your past and recent memories of being a learner also play a part. Some student teachers are particularly influenced by their experience of school and, like Paula below, trace their interest in teaching back to that:

> Even as a pupil at school I was observing how the teachers did it. I would come out of a lesson and think they did that well or that didn't work. On the whole I loved school and got involved in my subject there. You could look back and say I was heading for teaching. I knew a lot of other people didn't feel this way but I did and I remember a teacher I had, she really knew her subject and had time to build up individual relationships with us. I suppose she influenced me in wanting to become a teacher myself.

In contrast, some trace their interest by a desire to redress what they saw as their negative experience of school, as Peter confirms:

> An odd thing when I think about teaching was that I was never comfortable at school and felt bullied at times. Nothing serious in comparison with stories you hear but I never felt comfortable, and always wary. I think in my motivation to teach there is something there about wanting to put it right.

Focus questions

- What has motivated you to train to teach?
- How has your motivation to teach changed over the course of your training programme?
- What do you think is best going to sustain your motivation as a newly qualified teacher?

You and your changing views of teaching

Your motivation will have been stretched at times during your training and your view of the job will change as you come to understand what teaching involves. Adjusting your perspective on teaching can be very challenging and you will have worked hard to understand the different roles of the teacher, for example as both a controller of pupils and as an 'enabler' of pupils' learning.

Class management

One of the first difficulties you may have encountered was that of managing pupils. If you went into teaching to help young people by handing over knowledge and skills this might sit uneasily with ordering or directing pupils, no matter how much you may accept that this is a necessary part of the job. Jonathan explains:

> I knew why I wanted to teach and I had quite a lot of experience of youth work before I came to the course, but I was petrified just thinking about standing in front of a class of teenagers for the first time. When I first applied for the course I thought I would be OK but then the thought of 30 15-year-olds started to kick in! And then it creeps up on you . . . six weeks 'til I know what and where I am going to teach, five weeks 'til I know what I have to teach, four weeks and then it's tomorrow I've got to teach! And you do the lesson plan and the lesson goes nothing like it! You go off on a tangent, your hands are sweating and you can't even keep eye contact with the kids because you're so nervous. But even though I thought I was crap I also knew in a way that it went alright and it got better from there. So gradually I found the confidence to stand at the door and watch them come in and bark at them to get them settled, ask them questions and so on. It is slowly becoming second nature. Someone was watching me the other day and said, 'You are really managing this class well', and I thought, 'Yes, I guess I had cracked it.'

Jonathan was acutely conscious that pupils were expecting a measure of control and direction that, at least initially, he was unsure he could offer them. To use a simple analogy, it was as if he was in a play in which there was a role for him but he had trouble remembering the script. When he did recall his lines he could not speak them with conviction. Over time, and with the support of his mentor, the role became clearer and easier. This did not come so easily to other student teachers. Leah, for example, went into teacher training because she wanted to take the child's side in what seemed, in her own experience, to be an alien and intimidating world:

I realised more and more that I was uncomfortable with some aspects of the school. I did a pupil trail one day when I sat in on lessons with the same class. Seen through their eyes it just seemed to be shouting all the time, do this, do that. The whole system seems more to do with policing and management rather than creativity and I am not sure if I can fit into it at all. It is a real challenge to me to see how I can deal with the classes and hold on to why I went into this job in the first place.

Leah had sound reasons for deciding to teach but at times she felt it was enough to demonstrate, and go on demonstrating, her kindness and compassion, rather than reflect on what she could do to make the classroom a more productive environment for pupils to learn in. Teaching challenged and saddened her. She went on to become an excellent teacher but not in mainstream schooling.

Like Leah you might still be having difficulties adjusting to some of the demands of classroom management. You might think this is something that may yet defeat you. This is not a book about leaving teaching, but even at this late stage in your training you might still be thinking of career alternatives. There is no point in continuing to train for a career for which you do not feel suited (see research by Chambers and Roper 2000). However, the outlook need not be so gloomy. You might find it helpful to reassure yourself about what pupils are looking for from you as a teacher. Research findings (for example, Devereux 2001; Keys and Fernandes 1993) here are consistent. Yes, pupils are looking for an ordered classroom but they also want respect and encouragement, they rate very highly the teacher's ability to explain, the use of humour and the idea of justice. They are not looking for a despot but, rather, a 'firm but fair' teacher. There is room for creativity and individuality in how you manage pupils.

You will almost certainly find it helpful to talk over any worries you have about managing particular classes with mentors and colleagues. You might get a different perspective on what, at the moment, still seems overwhelmingly difficult. If you accept the importance of class management, and have come to terms with what pupils expect of you, you might want to look in practical terms at what you can do to create an orderly environment for teaching and learning. Some useful advice is included in Box 1.1. The point made strongly is that there is not a single recipe for managing a classroom and there are aspects of pupils' behaviour which are out of your control. However,

Box 1.1 Advice on class management

There are several very good text books on the issues of class management which feature on most training programmes. These include Kyriacou's *Essential Teaching Skills* (1992) which stresses that rewards for good behaviour set a positive environment for teaching and learning, and *You Know the Fair Rule* (Rogers 1997) which stresses the need for agreed rules of behaviour rather than the personalisation of conflict. *Class Management* (Wragg 1993) offers useful advice for primary teachers, but much crosses easily into the secondary sector. For example, the book stresses the importance of teacher 'withitness'. This means paying attention to what is going on in the whole class, communicating this to the pupils and picking up the signals so that you step in to prevent classroom challenges before they get out of hand. More recently, the DfES-sponsored national strategy at key stage 3 (pupils aged 11–14) focuses on behaviour and attendance (DfES 2003a). The strategy materials seek a sense of proportion, schools are not in crisis, most are well run, orderly places. However, serious incidents and continuous low-level challenge by pupils do reduce the morale of many teachers. The strategy argues that whole-school measures work and much of the material is geared around identifying the challenges faced in the school and devising appropriate solutions. Teachers are asked to look beyond the surface, to find out 'what is really going on'. This is not a question of devising more rules and regulations but being open about how the existing procedures are understood by teachers and pupils. As you will have found already, the strategy documents do not propose short-term solutions to pupil challenge in the classroom. However, progress can be made by more skilled management of behaviour; for example, stopping small incidents escalating into much larger ones, by being positive and by providing teachers with effective support. The strategy draws a link between pupil behaviour and effective teaching; for example, lessons that are accessible, relevant and interesting will reduce stress and challenge in class.

Many student teachers are dissatisfied with the advice they get on dealing with difficult pupils, but this is inevitable considering its general nature. No one can offer a guaranteed blueprint for what will work for you with this individual or this class in this school. Use the books, and whatever advice institutions may offer you, as suggestions but be aware that you might be experiencing difficulties for any of several different reasons. Try to diagnose these reasons and address them to the best of your ability. Focus carefully on what you can do to influence the class while being aware that some of the causes for pupil behaviour are out of your control.

Try to get a wider perspective on class management. Pupil conflict might be a general feature of a school, for example, arising from longstanding disaffection built up within low-achieving sets of pupils, your school might not be providing you with the support you need as a student teacher in working with these youngsters, or your school might not have a tradition of working with student teachers. Look to see how you might alter pupil perspectives on your teaching. You might have gaps in your communication skills, you might appear over fussy to pupils and create conflicts where none need to exist or where a more experienced teacher might let the issue resolve itself. Alternatively, you might be perceived and resented as too lax, and almost certainly lacking confidence. Inadvertently you may have created a mood in which pupils feel they can get away with things they would not be able to do, or even think of doing, elsewhere in school.

Sometimes, pupil challenge is part and parcel of a process of pupil testing which will fade with time. Difficulties in the classroom might be rooted in inappropriate planning that fails to provide an entry point to pupils, many of whom become unmotivated and sullen as a result, or a lack of variety that leaves pupils bored and restless. Whatever suggestions you have concerning pupils' behaviour will need to compete with school and teacher folklore, much of dubious value: 'they are always like this on Wednesday afternoon', 'never expect boys to work with girls', 'never allow single-sex groups', 'don't expect too much of them', 'don't leave them bored', 'it's all in their hormones' and so on.

You may be acutely aware of the emotional turmoil caused by challenging pupils, but try somehow to step back from the problem. This is easier said than done, but keep in mind that there is a lot more going on in pupils' lives than you and your teaching; their frustration is not directed at you personally. Be open about your difficulties with your friends and close colleagues with whom you are carrying out your training. They can help you see things in a wider perspective. At school an essential strategy is to talk things through with your mentors and get repeated observations of your teaching. Draw on the advice offered in books and on the support available in school. Develop your own diagnosis of the problem, share it with others and discuss possible ways of addressing it. Test these out in the classroom. If the problem seems to you to lie in the make-up of the class ask for support but have realistic expectations, recognise the sensitivity of the situation, look for opportunities to accentuate the positive and be prepared to tough it out. As suggested by Rogers, stay calm, refer to a set of classroom rules and try to avoid personalising your comments or overreacting. To address your communication skills rehearse very carefully what you are going to say, including the questions you are going to ask, get precise advice on where you should stand in the room, how your voice carries and so on. You will want to get feedback on how you come over in the classroom. The more you can rehearse the better because you will find it very difficult to 'think on your feet' in front of the class if you are feeling stressed.

Of course, classroom problems are rarely the result of a single cause, and over time you will need to build up a picture of each individual in the class. Accept that you are having to address more than one problem. Try not to focus solely on control, for example the greater use of sanctions such as detentions and withdrawals of pupils and the more visible support of other teachers. At the same time, rethink your planning to better meet the interests of your pupils, your whole-class teaching and the way you work with individual pupils.

there are strategies and approaches which have worked for others and which are worth trying and may work for you.

As you gain confidence in managing the class you will have had more time to consider the complexity of what is being asked of you in supporting pupil learning. Like many other student teachers, Ahmed confessed he had rather naive views on teaching at first but had been quick to realise what would be expected of him as a teacher:

> My first thoughts about teaching were based on what I had been through. I thought, in a normal classroom, it is the teacher at the front telling them what to do. Simple as that. But when you get in there yourself you find it's completely different. Although you do stand up and teach them at the beginning you are then constantly going around checking on what they are doing and trying to assess the different abilities of each child. It is very draining, there are so many that need your help and so little time for each one.

Ahmed draws attention to a very important shift of focus from himself as a teacher to the pupils and their learning. When you started teaching you may have concentrated on your own performance, and were perhaps very aware of your shortcomings, but over time you may have become less self-conscious and more aware of what pupils are learning. Krysia found this change of focus difficult:

> I look back on the first days and wonder why I could get it so out of proportion. Every lesson had to be so good and I had to get everything just right. If they did not get it, I felt it was my fault. I flew around the room every lesson. I stayed behind after lessons and was always there for them after school if they wanted to see me. But it dawned on me that it couldn't be like this all the time, it wasn't all about me. It was about what I had planned for them to do and how they reacted to it.

Krysia was able to discuss her teaching with her mentor and together they worked out strategies for getting pupils to help and support each other more. Krysia needed to support pupils but to hold back sometimes, to give them time to flounder and work things out for themselves.

Some student teachers talked about events that helped them see the subject from the pupils' point of view. Daniel, a history teacher, explained:

I guess I went into teaching history as it seemed the next best thing to an academic career. I love my subject and there have been real highs in getting to know more about it and sharing ideas with the pupils, particularly the sixth form. There are some really bright ones and you can get them to think about different perspectives on history. But it all seems a bit wasted on the younger ones. It came to a head with me when I was teaching the Y9s about the First World War. I knew all about this as I had specialised in it for university. I could reel off the key events, the different interpretations, the implications of the war and so on. And then suddenly in the class someone asks me how many people died in the war. I didn't know. OK it was a good question but I didn't know and I felt foolish. I could guess and I could find out easily enough but that's not the point. It was a child's question, not how does this affect this or that view of the First World War but simple curiosity. I thought then and there I am going to have to see things from the child's point of view a bit more, find a way of starting from where they start.

This event led to a very important adjustment in Daniel's teaching. He was understandably proud of his own knowledge of his subject but he could not know everything. In any case, what he knew was only going to be any good if he could make it accessible to the children he was teaching. With guidance and support, he began to develop an approach to teaching that gave pupils more opportunities to talk about their own understanding of a topic before being directed into an activity. He began to see his role as helping pupils ask questions about the past and pointing them to resources, many ICT-based, where they might find answers. He felt more relaxed if there were gaps in his own knowledge as these indicated avenues that pupils could take in their own research.

Focus question

- How has your view of teaching changed over the course of your training programme? What or who has led you to adjust your views?

Expressing yourself in your teaching

It is clearly important to adjust to the expectations of colleagues and pupils but the trick, or one of the tricks, in learning to teach is to hold on to your very personal view of your role while being prepared to adapt to the expectations of others. Give two teachers the same lesson to teach and they will do it in very different ways. This is because, as teachers, we need to draw on our own intuition about how pupils think and learn and what we believe is the proper role of the teacher.

Your intuition about teaching may be rooted in the 'apprentice-ship' you yourself had as a pupil and you may set out, whether consciously or not, to emulate the people who taught you. However, your relationship with your past schooling is likely to be complex. Some find it easy to talk about teachers who they almost see as role models for their teaching but, earlier, Peter described how he had gone into teaching almost to address his negative experience of school and was influenced by his teachers only in the sense that he wanted to do much better. Some student teachers see experiences of work-placed learning, or participation in voluntary groups, as far greater influences on their teaching than anything that went on at school.

All kinds of memories of teaching and learning play a part in how you teach, even if you are not always fully aware of them. For example, when you plan a lesson you are right to see yourself as making sensible and considered choices on what to teach, how you are going to teach it and how you are going to assess what pupils have learnt. However, key decisions about the lesson, including levels of direction and control, are likely to be heavily influenced by some taken-for-granted assumptions about the way pupils think and learn. The writer Bruner calls these 'folk pedagogies' and he closely links them to our assumptions about children. He suggests some think of children as naturally naughty and needing to be controlled, while some believe children are oppressed and need to express themselves. Many simply think of children as malleable and there to be won over. When it comes to teaching and learning Bruner suggests that there are four dominant folk pedagogies (Bruner 1996). The first views children as 'imitative' and the job of the teacher as one of passing on skills and 'know-how' through practical demonstration. The second sees children as needing explanations as well as demonstrations; there are concepts or rules that children need to learn, remember and apply. The third takes much greater account of children as creative thinkers. The teacher will want to understand how the child makes sense of his or her world and encourage the child to understand, and reach consensus, on other views of the world. Such a teacher will value discussion and collaboration. The fourth views children as already knowing a great deal about the world but needing to access knowledge that society has accumulated over a great deal of time. Again, the teacher will value creativity and collaboration but will want to show pupils what society views as important knowledge. The first two of these approaches to teaching and learning have a stronger focus on the teacher, the second on the creativity of the pupils. The distinctions between these folk pedagogies are quite subtle but you might consider where you fit, if at all, within this picture by way of simply analogy. If teaching is a journey would you be:

- a demonstrator: for example, would you show pupils how to read a map and then set off with them following you?
- a teller: for example, would you sit pupils down and explain to them the principles of map making and map reading, provide them with various examples to practise and then take them out on a trip?
- an explorer: for example, would you set off on the journey, talk with pupils about what they see and encourage them to draw, share and refine their own maps of the journey?
- a guide: for example, would you set off on the journey, swap notes on what you all see but point out the various building and features that cartographers have considered important enough to mark out for them?

You are, of course, unlikely to fit neatly into one of these categories but you will have your own assumptions about teaching. These may be both helpful and inhibiting. They are helpful in that they give you a personal orientation to teaching and a framework for how to plan work and how to act in the classroom. You may also find that as these assumptions are very much based on what worked for you as a learner they might, by extension, provide you with a reliable guide to what works for other learners. As Carlton, an ICT teacher, explains:

> When I think about what would interest youngsters in learning ICT the first thing I think about is what would I make of it if it was me. I think about the things I liked to do with computers and how I got into using computers at home. You had to have

a problem you wanted to solve or something that you wanted to do and there was a lot of playing about at the machine until you got there. There was a lot of help and sharing ideas from texting or talking to mates. When I was in school the good teachers gave me time to work at what I wanted to do but talked to me and knew when was the right time to show me something or have me think about what I was doing. I try to think about teaching in the same way, so I guess my assumptions about teaching are give them problems to work on, give them time to sort themselves out, then talk to them if they are going wrong and share ideas about what we are doing. It seems to work very well.

Carlton developed a much wider view of his role over his training programme but his initial assumption stood him in good stead. He saw himself as a 'guide' for pupils, a very skilful guide, who knew when to stand back and when to intervene. It was a style of working that appealed to the particular pupils he was teaching though he was not always aware that there were pupils who may have responded better to a more structured approach.

In contrast, Stacey, a science teacher, was someone who gravitated towards the role of the teacher as 'teller' based on her own experience of teaching and learning:

The thing about science is that most people think it is doing experiments but when I look back it was the ones who could explain ideas and build stories around what we were doing who could help me most. One example, we did this whole thing on antibiotics and penicillin built around Alexander Fleming and how he had left some used culture plates unattended for several weeks. You probably know the story, he arrived back from his vacation to find fungus growing on them: on one plate, the bacteria he was working with had not taken hold as he thought it would because by accident there was some of the Penicillin fungus. Anyway, he not only told the story, he explained the science as he went on and brought us up to date with resistance to bacteria and what was happening now. Things like this not only got me interested but helped me understand the science involved.

Stacey instinctively understood the power of story telling and the role of the teacher in explaining ideas in lively and accessible settings. Like Carlton she was encouraged to develop a more rounded approach to teaching but her vivid and imaginative explanations were always a strength of her teaching.

In contrast, your intuition about teaching and learning becomes inhibiting when you feel overcommitted to one way of working and one belief in how pupils think and learn. For example, we saw that Maria held to a view of pupils being oppressed and a strong belief that her role was to explore knowledge with them. She may have been right or wrong to hold these beliefs; the problem was that she found it difficult to understand the demands pupils made on her. Stephen faced a similar problem. He was similarly committed to seeing teaching as exploration and used 'active learning' in his teaching based on his own experiences as both a learner and an industry trainer:

> I really felt that active learning is important in doing English. Children are so passive in school, I want them to think about what they are doing, take risks, learn from each other. I don't want them glued in front of a book all day. So I came in with this frame of mind. In practice it did not work out, in fact it ended in chaos. I put pupils together but they argued and mucked about. I was determined to stick with it. Eventually, my mentor said, 'Look at what is happening, don't just go on doing the same thing, ask yourself why it is happening and what you can do about it.'

In Stephen's case it was not enough to be committed to a style of working, he needed to think about the consequences of his teaching for pupils' learning. There is nothing wrong with active learning approaches, and plenty to commend giving pupils opportunities for talking together – Neil Mercer, for example, in several articles and books, has discussed different aspects of pupils' talk and the power of dialogue to 'scaffold' learning (Mercer 1995, 2000). However, in his zeal, Stephen had not considered how to organise pupils. He had not set clear guidelines. This was especially important as pupils were being asked to try something new. Over time, Stephen did succeed in adjusting his teaching style but it was a long process and required considerable support. In his case (and compare with guidance from, for example, DfES 2003b) he became much more directed in his teaching without forsaking the idea of pupil collaboration. Instead of simply asking pupils to discuss ideas together, he explained, and tried to enforce, the ground rules by which pupils should work; for example, that they should listen to each other, they should take turns in speaking, they should respond constructively to what others said. He gave and discussed key phrases they could use to express disagreement. He became much more directed in putting pupils in certain groups and gave much more tightly focused tasks, for example to agree on a list of the three most important traits of a character in a book. He set time limits on how long pupils should work together and learnt to organise much more concise feedback from each group.

Your intuition about teaching and learning, then, is a helpful guide to working with pupils, but a guide that needs to be amended and updated in the light of experience. Very much the same can be said about working with colleagues in the department in which you are carrying out your training. For example, your training will be made much easier if you are working in a department that shares your ideas about teaching. As Judith commented on the art department in her placement school:

> What I liked about the department was that they felt quite happy about demonstrating techniques to children. I think I was worried that they would see art as only about creativity and expressing yourself – and of course all this is very important. But there are things you can show children and things they should practise and I just felt I fitted in with what they did.

In contrast, you might feel quite alienated from some of the approaches taken with your school, as in Leah's case discussed earlier. If this is true for you, try to use the experience of your placement to guide you in your choice of school for next year. (Appendix A at the back of the book gives advice on choosing your first school, which you may find it useful even if you have accepted a job already.) Try to understand the perspectives your colleagues have on teaching. Can you identify any strengths in the way they approach teaching? What can you learn from them? You might look back and find some of your initial thinking about your department was naive. But do not lose sight of the critical insight you had when you first went into school. You have a fresh perspective on teaching and learning which you want to develop, not lose. As Sue explains:

> When I came in I thought all these schemes were just boring the children. They did not want to do them and I couldn't blame them. Well I tried it and realise it is not so easy. Now I realise much more why things are done in a certain way, there are after all 30 people and you cannot have them doing their own thing,

there is a syllabus to get through and there needs to be some sense of control over them. There is not time to plan interesting events for every class, sometimes they just need to jump through the hoops in the textbook. But I hope I haven't lost my enthusiasm for teaching and I want to stick at making changes when and where I can.

Focus questions

- How do you believe pupils think and learn?
- How have you had to readjust your beliefs about teaching and learning over the course of your training programme?
- How are you hoping to express your beliefs as a teacher in your next school?
- How easily do you think you are going to fit into your next school?

Summary

This chapter has looked at:

- your motivation to teach;
- your changing views of teaching;
- expressing yourself in your teaching.

Chapter 2

Strengths and areas to develop in your teaching

The previous chapter considered your motivation to teach and your personal contribution to teaching. This chapter focuses more specifically on what you do well as a teacher and areas for development. The chapter will help you:

- identify your strengths as a teacher;
- identify areas to develop in your teaching;
- consider your training programme in a wider context.

Your strengths as a teacher

At various times during your training you will probably have been asked to describe your strengths as a teacher. An exercise like this can boost your self-confidence and help you plan your career development. The sections below illustrate how some student teachers were able to develop and describe their strengths. These are categorised under knowledge and understanding; planning; assessing; and classroom teaching, broadly in line with the standards approach to which they were working (*Qualifying to Teach* (QtT), TTA 2003a – professional values feature strongly within these standards but are taken as implicit within the examples). These sections provide a snapshot of individual teachers; you may well have other strengths not described here.

Knowledge and understanding

Three important aspects of subject knowledge concern subject matter, pedagogical content and curricular knowledge (Shulman 1986). Subject matter refers to your knowledge of your subject in its widest sense, not just the key concepts and ideas but knowledge of the controversies and debates and a sense of how the subject evolves over time. Pedagogical content refers to your knowledge of how the subject can be explained or made comprehensible to others and what makes the learning of specific topics easy or difficult. Finally, curricular knowledge refers to what you know about particular teaching programmes and the materials used in them. It is useful to differentiate subject knowledge in this way because you may have strengths in one area of subject knowledge but not another. For example, in Chapter 1 we saw that Daniel started his course with very good knowledge of subject matter in history but much less-developed knowledge of pedagogical content. In a similar way, Peter, a teacher of mathematics, needed to develop both his curricular and pedagogical content knowledge over the course of his placement:

> The challenge for me was getting on top of the exam courses. You think you know the subject as you spent long enough learning about it but you realise it is a different matter teaching it. You need to know what they (the pupils) are expected to cover and what the examiners are looking for in the course work they produce and in the exams they sit. By the end of the placement I felt that I knew the framework we were teaching to. It wasn't just knowing more about the topics, it was having a model of the kind of work the exam board was expecting and what differentiated work at different grades. I remember pupils asking me how they should do one of the exam questions and that would have stumped me first time round. But now I could find the right explanation and get them started on it.

You may find it helpful to identify your strengths in relation to these three areas of subject knowledge and to consider whether Shulman's categories match the descriptions of knowledge and understanding within your training programme.

Planning

You will have been given particular advice on planning within your training programme. Some of the more generic issues covered include the importance of being explicit in your learning objectives ('we are learning to') and outcomes ('what I am looking for') and how these aims and objectives fit into a wider scheme of work (for example,

DfES 2003c). You will have looked at planning pedagogical approaches around learning objectives. For example, if pupils are going to investigate a relationship between variables or consider their own emotional responses to a text then they will need an exploratory approach with opportunities to make choices in how they address a task or activity. On the other hand, if you want pupils to practise certain skills then your planning will include teacher demonstration and modelling and early feedback on pupil performance. A lesson plan will include a 'recipe' – activities such as starters, main activities and plenaries with timings and points of transition. Planning might involve you designing your own teaching material, but even if you are relying on existing material you will want to prepare and rehearse your explanations of key terms and your directions to pupils. A key consideration as you reach the end of your training programme is to use your assessment of pupils in your planning, for example, to consider differentiation, learning styles and special needs within the class.

Do you have strengths in an area of planning? One place to start is looking at positive learning outcomes in the classroom and track back to the planning that helped achieve these outcomes. Janet, for example, realised she was someone who could motivate low achievers and associated this with her patience, her positive manner and spending time to get to know individuals:

> I found the children in the school were just so keen. It's a great boost when you see them doing well but the main thing is when you see a kid that's not doing too well and you help them out. What they really want is some attention, some way into the topic and someone to make it clear to them what they have to do. You can actually see their development and that's fantastic.

Janet's positive attitude to low-achieving pupils is important but there was more to her teaching than this. Through discussion with her mentor she became more aware of the planning that went into her work. For example, she found 'pupil friendly' ways of describing the aims of the lesson and rehearsed her explanations of key words and concepts in order to make these as clear as possible. She planned to finish lessons with plenaries involving simple crosswords and quizzes that reinforced key words and encouraged pupils to reflect on what they had learnt. A strength inside the classroom was just as much a strength in planning.

Another teacher, Pranav, identified a strength in planning – in his case working with pupils with English as an additional language. He was able to draw on his own knowledge of community languages inside the classroom but this did not detract him from preparing suitable support material in advance of the lesson:

> There were little things which really helped some pupils make progress, like I could use some Punjabi in classes from time to time to help them when they were obviously struggling with a key word or instruction. I could see the problems some of the pupils were having with explanations and I spent time, a lot of time, thinking about the pictures and diagrams I could use in my worksheets and in my boardwork. I was lucky in that I could use an overhead display with this class and I could download lots of pictures and the odd video clip onto the computer to illustrate anything I wanted to say. When I look back on the ways some of my pupils got involved in the lesson, I think, yes my sensitivity to language, and my planning in making language as clear as possible, that is a strength of mine.

Assessment

Assessment refers to anything that provides feedback for you and your pupils. Key terms discussed in nearly all training programmes are formative assessment (assessment for learning) and summative assessment (assessment of learning). A strength in formative assessment might include feeling comfortable with a range of approaches, for example scanning the class, observing particular pupils, marking work, question and answer with pupils, plenary activities, and an awareness of how each approach contributes to your understanding of your pupils' progress. A strength within summative assessment might refer to your ability to assess against national curriculum levels or against key criteria within a qualification course. You might also have strengths in reporting on pupils, for example to parents.

Strengths in assessment are of little value unless you and your pupils can act on feedback. For example, Corrine, a science teacher, recounts a breakthrough in her teaching – a particular strength of the activity she describes lay in its appeal to the 'kinaesthetic' learner (Smith 1996; Gardner 1993) – and the role of assessment within it:

In a university session we talked about this idea that we could get the pupils to act out being molecules and what happened to them as the temperature rose. The class needed to stand up and gather round, all bunched together and you told them they were getting hotter so they needed to move apart, and as they cooled down they would bunch together again. I was very nervous about doing this with my class, but when I did I could see that they really got into it – even those who were normally not interested. And it was not just about having fun. I quizzed them on it afterwards and I could see that they had grasped the ideas, I could use that to move them on to the next bit of the lesson. At the end of the lesson I asked them what they thought of the activity and they said they had enjoyed it. So I thought there is something there I could use next time. I needed to find something to get everyone involved, not just those who stick up their hand and offer an answer.

In this lesson the role of assessment was twofold. First, Corrine used formative assessment of pupils (no more than question and answer) to check pupils' understanding and act on what she had learnt to move the lesson on. Second, she carried out an assessment of her planning and teaching, through scanning the class and talking to pupils at the end of the lesson. She drew the conclusion that the activity had motivated pupils and used this to inform the planning of her next lesson. She was seeing teaching as a cycle of planning, teaching and assessment, with assessment feeding back into planning. This is a recurring theme within teacher development and will be discussed further in Chapter 3.

Another teacher, Jasbir, illustrates the twofold nature of assessment in introducing a loop game in his lesson:

In one class I wanted them to think about the key words so we did this loop game. Each person had a key word and a definition of a key word, not their one, to go with it. What happened is one pupil starts with a definition and whoever has the key word pipes up. They then give the definition on their card. The person with that key word speaks up and on and on in a loop. The thing is they really enjoyed it and I could see they were thinking about what they had learnt. I would not have done this first time round as I felt it would not have worked, but now I had them all sitting round and they wanted to do it again and again – it was brilliant. It was valuable learning for them but it also really worked for me. I could see what they did not grasp so well and what I would need to talk about again next time.

Over the course of his placement Jasbir developed other plenary activities in a game style format which gave further opportunities for formative assessment. These enabled pupils to reflect on their learning as well as enabling him to reflect on his teaching – again, this was feedback he could use for future planning.

Teaching and class management

A third aspect of your teaching concerns your pedagogic skills in action inside the classroom, for example your ability not just to plan but carry out interactive whole-class teaching, to demonstrate and explain concepts, to manage behaviour in the classroom, to use ICT confidently and to work collaboratively with specialist teachers and other colleagues.

The previous chapter described student teachers' difficulties when taking control of a class. Most settled into this role and for some class management became a strength. For example, Claire was a student teacher who fretted about her control of a class during most of her placement. However, she worked hard to establish classroom routines with her pupils resulting in a more orderly environment in which pupils could learn:

> It seem silly to say it but what is a strength in my teaching is the boring things like getting them into the habit of listening to each other, having them listening to me, tracking their homework, being on top of the marking. It makes me sound dull and predictable but yes it is a strength in my teaching.

The 'boring bits' that Claire describes included simple procedures such as managing pupils' entry into the classroom, not starting the lesson until everyone was quiet, explaining the aims of the lesson to pupils and recapping points arising out of the lesson at the end. Claire undervalued these elements of her teaching as she liked to think of herself as a lively and innovative teacher. She benefited from discussing these aspects of teaching with a mentor and came to see that there was no contradiction between routine and innovation – as she became more settled in her classroom routines she became more confident in planning more innovative work with the pupils.

Another example of a strength in classroom teaching concerned Jane's use of ICT in teaching history. She became aware of this as a strength when asked to contribute to a departmental meeting:

> I really got into ICT at school. There were much better facilities there than I had imagined and I was able to book one of the computer rooms quite often. One of the teachers in the department was really encouraging and had done quite a lot of work himself. With his help I got into looking at what a census database told us about how people lived in the past and we did a newspaper simulation exercise reporting on a mining disaster in the 1860s. We had done quite a lot of work on web sites at university and I was able to show him the video clips which you could get over the internet and I got pupils to use them in their presentations. I think he was surprised by how much there was out there which you can use in our subject and I felt that it wasn't all one way, he was giving me advice but I was putting something back. My mentor got me to do a session with all the teachers in the department on the ICT work I had done. This put me on the spot but it was good, I think they could see I wasn't being competitive. I just showed them some things and told them how the pupils had responded and some of the work they had done. This confirmed for me that I had a strength in working with ICT.

Using ICT gave Jane a boost in confidence and helped her feel she had made a special contribution to the department. She saw ICT as motivating her pupils and giving them access to activities they could not easily do otherwise – a view for which there is some support in recent reports on the impact of ICT on pupils' learning (Comber *et al.* 2002; Harrison *et al.* 2002; Somekh *et al.* 2002).

Identifying strengths

You may find little difficulty in recognising your own strengths, but this is not always the case. Sometimes you may be unaware of them, take them for granted, find them difficult to describe. This was certainly the case for the teachers described above who found it helpful to identify their strengths through:

- discussing their work with mentors or tutors;
- considering the impact of what they were doing for pupils' learning (e.g. were pupils more motivated, more focused, better able to grasp learning objectives?);
- noting special knowledge, experience or values they brought into the classroom;
- contrasting their performance with other teachers in the department, or with their own earlier performance;
- picking out approaches or attitudes that worked in different classes;
- referencing what they were doing to curriculum models they had read about or seen.

The teachers later talked about the confidence they gained in identifying strengths and how it 'freed' them up to focus on other areas of their teaching.

For you to do

With the help of a colleague or mentor identify three or four strengths in your teaching and explain why these strengths contribute to pupil learning. Think about different aspects of your teaching, say, your planning, class management and your assessment. Highlight examples of strengths in each category and discuss the evidence which backs up claims about your strengths.

Areas for development in your teaching

As with your strengths you will have been asked to identify areas of development throughout your training programme. Perhaps you are more conscious of these than your strengths but it is still important to discuss them with others to get a clearer perspective on your teaching. Below are some examples of student teachers who identified areas for development and took steps to address them. Again, they cover aspects of planning, subject knowledge, teaching and assessment. They are only a sample of a wide range of issues that you might face as a student teacher.

Planning – lack of variety

This example contrasts with that of Corrine's lesson discussed earlier. Chris, like many student teachers towards the end of their training programme, felt confident in teaching to the 'three part' lesson – whole-class introduction, largely independent pupil activity and whole-class plenary. It was difficult for him to see the need to broaden his range of teaching styles:

> I thought I was doing very well in my teaching as I had good control over the class and was pleased with the progress they were making, so I was a bit shocked when my tutor said there was still a long way to go. He wanted me to make more use of role play and group work ideas which I found a bit scary. But it was a fair point; all he was saying was that the same thing will not appeal to everyone and I could not teach every lesson in the same way.

It would have been easy for Chris to coast through the final stages of his placement, but instead, with support, he was able to try out new approaches in his teaching. For example, he developed his use of group work, albeit within a very structured approach along guidelines suggested by his mentor.

Teaching – providing clear explanations

In Chapter 1, Sue described the importance of contextualising the discovery of penicillin within a story which pupils could be drawn into. In contrast Dean, a technology teacher, describes how he became aware of the difficulties pupils had in accessing his explanations and only with time did he begin to reflect on ways in which he could improve this aspect of his teaching:

> During the course we had done some peer teaching with colleagues from different subjects. There was a geography student who made an impression as he was explaining about weather patterns. The thing was I knew nothing and cared very little about this as a topic. But his explanation was really good. He held up an inflated balloon and let go of it, it zipped around the class and he explained air under pressure would escape rapidly if released. There needed to be a balance between the pressure inside the balloon and that within the atmosphere. That was why air

pressure was important in predicting weather patterns – you get high pressure, then you get greater wind speeds. The point is that this difficult concept was made very clear to me and to be honest I don't think I have reached the same clarity in my work or when I look in lessons in this department I don't think I have seen much that has impressed me.

In discussion with his tutor, Dean came to see that explanations which he gave pupils were too abstract. Pupils had a superficial understanding of what he was saying. They could follow instructions, but they could not adequately explain the work they were doing. In order to make his explanations more accessible Dean needed to put them in a context to which they could relate. The point with the balloon example was that Dean's colleague took a simple context that everyone understood and had experienced and used it to explain an idea that was abstract and difficult. The lesson successfully bridged the gap between Dean's world and the world of the subject specialist. Dean was encouraged to work on his explanations of key terms in his planning and demonstrate more carefully crafted explanations in his teaching. Not surprisingly, given that he lacked effective models in his department, he struggled. However, he was able to come up with some more vivid explanations to pupils and appreciated better the misconceptions that pupils might have.

Classroom management

A common starting point in thinking through areas to develop is to consider your worries and low points in learning to teach. Many almost certainly focus on the conflicts with pupils. These may more often be low-level interruptions such as talking when trying to get attention at the beginning of class, pupils being flippant when you are asking them to get on with some work or contribute to a discussion, their reluctance to work together on a group activity, and the constant need to focus attention. Not surprisingly this is wearying and, like many others, Chris found his confidence and motivation to teach undermined:

> Yeah, the worst thing about teaching are the kids in that school. Not all of them but in every class there's ones that I never got on with, always disruptive, always talking. They would never do their work and it was just constantly detention after detention.

You end up getting worked up and shouting all the time, which I don't like doing, and is not why I went into it in the first place.

Class management remained a critical area of development for Chris throughout his placement. He discussed various strategies to address this with his mentor. Some seemed fairly straightforward to identify, such as remembering and using names of pupils in his class and making sure he followed through on classroom rules. He was urged to focus sanctions on individual pupils and not the whole class, for example to avoid statements such as 'if you don't stop messing about you are all coming back'. He was inadvertently egging on difficult pupils by talking about his reaction to their behaviour ('if you don't stop doing that then I will be very angry') rather than the consequences for their learning ('if you don't stop doing that then you won't understand what you have to do'). He was not monitoring the whole class by looking up and scanning what was going on. More difficult to address was planning. He was encouraged to think carefully about the balance inside a lesson, perhaps to reduce the length of time he expected pupils to listen to him and to use that time more effectively to demonstrate or model activities as clearly as possible. He tried to think of more engaging activities for pupils, but not to create tension in the class by being over ambitious. The support of the mentor was crucial for Chris to address this challenge in his teaching.

Lack of experience

Areas of development are usually identified through reflecting on your work in the classroom but sometimes they may refer to areas in which you simply lack experience. Two frequently occurring examples cover ICT and teaching examination classes.

Using ICT

Many student teachers, like Jane described earlier, come to a training programme with basic or even good ICT skills and can come up with some interesting ideas for using ICT in their teaching. However, they often find limited opportunities and limited encouragement to try out ideas in the classroom. Here, for example, Hope looks back on constraints in using ICT:

We did a lot of work on using ICT in RE in college and I was very keen to use it when I started at school. It took me a while to find the courage to try to book the IT room and then it was often block booked by other teachers when I wanted to use it. No one in the department seemed to be pushing me to use it and it all seemed too much bother. So, yes, this is one area I would like to develop next year.

Like Hope you might find the odds are stacked against you in developing some aspects of your work, particularly, as in this case, if this involves going outside your department to get access to equipment. However, try to be more assertive in this situation. For example, you could explain that there is a course requirement for you to use ICT and be persistent in using the machines, either those within a computer room or in a subject teaching area. In some schools the department may have access to its mini network or portable machines that you can use.

Getting access is only one dimension to planning (Hammond 2004) and, among other considerations, you might want to think about:

- whether pupils need to, or would benefit, from pairing up at machines;
- your own ICT knowledge and skills;
- where to get help during the lesson;
- what you expect the software to help pupils achieve.

Teaching of examination classes

A consistent difficulty within some training programmes is access to exam classes, for example GCSE and A level groups. Some classroom teachers are understandably reluctant to allow you to take over these classes with high-profile exams about to take place – and with such a lot of testing in school, high-profile exams are always about to take place! As Matt explains:

I was looking forward to knowing more about post-16 classes and doing some teaching but to be honest I did not get the chance. I sat in on a couple of lessons but I did not learn a lot from them and did not feel very welcome, so this is another gap in my teaching.

Faced with this situation, again, try to be more assertive than Matt but be sensitive to the pressure on schools and creative in suggesting solutions. For example, rather than simply observe a lesson negotiate a specific role; for example, offer to work with a group of students who appear to need extra support. Even at this late stage in your training programme you may have opportunities to offer to support or teach special revision sessions. Show colleagues you understand their concern for their pupils' exam performance and suggest you would like to team teach a topic. Choose a topic in which you feel confident and discuss your planning with the class teacher. Check that you have understood the course requirements. There are no guarantees here but many student teachers find initial reluctance from classroom teachers is overcome once they have demonstrated good subject knowledge and communicated that they have understood the impact of examination results on the profile of the department and the school. Clearly, if you are training to teach at key stages 3 and 4 only, there may be special issues in getting access to sixth form classes, particularly if you are working in an 11–16 school. However, you will benefit enormously from expanding your experience of teaching and you might suggest a short placement, or regular observations, of sixth form teaching in another institution. In contrast, if your training is in a 14–19 school you will want to get key stage 3 experience.

Identifying areas to develop

The teachers in these examples identified areas to develop in a broadly similar way to how they identified their strengths, though this time the focus was on how their practice fell short of their aspirations. They were able to:

- contrast their performance with other members of the department or other teachers;
- realise that progression in their teaching was slow or not taking place;
- compare what they were doing with other curriculum models;
- identify areas in which they lacked experience;
- discuss their teaching with mentors and tutors;
- reflect that pupils were not focused or not making appropriate progress in their lesson.

Areas of development often affected teachers' self-esteem and high-lighted priorities in development of teaching.

For you to do

With the help of a colleague or mentor identify three or four areas to develop in your teaching. Think about different aspects of your teaching, say, your planning, class management and your assessment. Discuss ideas for addressing these areas to develop.

A note on standards

In the above examples, strengths and areas to develop could be easily referenced to the particular standards that a training programme is designed to meet (in England, the QtT standards referenced earlier). This has not been done as descriptions of standards tend to change over time. However, at this point you may want to reflect on the purpose of following a standards-related approach in the first place.

Many student teachers saw considerable value in having QtT standards set out. These standards helped them focus on specific aspects of the job of the teacher; for example, questioning, differentiation, assessment for learning, use of group work. The standards often helped them set realistic goals. They felt there was probably a close match between the standards and what they intuitively felt about teaching, and some saw a match between the research literature and the standards see a report sponsored by the DfES into what makes an effective teacher (Hay McBer 2000).

However, many also became aware of the limitations of these standards. For example, the standards lacked any reference to context. It was all well and proper to aspire to, say, use questioning effectively but what did this mean and would it always be applied in the same way? There was, for example, a different level of challenge, calling on different strategies, in working with pupils in different classes, let alone different schools. Any assessment against the standards would, the student teachers felt, require a great deal of subjective interpretation.

Perhaps a bigger criticism of the standards approach was that it could lead student teachers to focus on individual aspects of teaching and not the whole picture – or how knowledge and skills 'come together' (Tomlinson 1995). Some also found the language to describe teaching rather flat – would you really want to describe inspiring teachers as, say, 'having high expectations' or 'establishing a purposeful learning environment where diversity is valued and where pupils feel secure and confident' as in the present QtT standards?

There are two important points about the standards approach. First, it is embedded into the culture of teacher assessment and performance management and, for better or worse, you cannot get away from it. Second, if the standards are going to be helpful you will need to see them as pointers and not simple rules about effective teaching. Try to be clear about how you understand words such as 'effective', 'high expectations' and 'purposeful', and ask those observing you to be explicit about how they interpret a standard and how your performance measures up to their interpretation. Put yourself in the position of applying the standards for yourself in observations of other teachers. Most training programmes feature a moderation exercise in which a whole class tries to apply the standards while watching a video of a student teacher's lesson. (The TTA has in the past produced materials to help with this kind of exercise and it is worth going to the TTA web site at www.tta.gov.uk for updates.) The standards approach helps when it promotes dialogue and helps you understand your development as a teacher and to articulate your achievements and concerns. In contrast, it is unhelpful when it leads to a checklist approach, when your teaching is assessed against descriptions that neither you, nor probably your tutor or mentor, fully understand, but which are seen as objective and unchallengeable (see Gilroy and Wilcox 1997 and comments by Drever and Cope 1999).

Your training programme in a wider context

You may be interested in comparing your experiences to those of student teachers and NQTs as described in two major reports on learning to teach in England (TTA 2003a; OFSTED 2003). Both reports are positive about the training of new teachers but highlight possible areas for development.

TTA survey

Every year since 2000 the TTA has surveyed newly qualified teachers (NQTs), seeking their views about the quality of their initial teacher training (ITT) and how well their training has prepared them for their first teaching post. For example, in 2003 the questionnaire was completed by more than 10,000 NQTs across both the primary and secondary sectors, a response rate of around 50 per cent.

In 2002 the vast majority of new teachers (86 per cent) rated the overall quality of their training as good or very good. There was little variation in response between male and female, those teaching different age ranges or by age. The widest variation came from subject background at secondary level, with history teachers being the most positive about their training – a staggering 93 per cent rating this as good or very good. Around three-quarters of respondents rated highly the quality of assessment from their training provider and the support and guidance they received. A large proportion of NQTs also thought their training was good or very good in:

- helping them understand the National Curriculum (78 per cent);
- providing them with the relevant knowledge, skills and understanding to teach their specialist subject (74 per cent);
- helping them to use teaching methods that promote pupils' learning (73 per cent).

The good news you can take from this survey is that your training programme might very well have prepared you to meet the challenge of your first year. If, in contrast, you have major concerns about your training programme then, even at this late stage, discuss these with your tutors and mentors.

The survey does, however, show variations in how NQTs rated other aspects of their training. In particular, they were less positive about the extent to which their training prepared them:

- for working with children with English as an additional language (20 per cent rating this as good or very good);
- for teaching pupils from minority ethnic groups (30 per cent);
- for teaching children with special educational needs (43 per cent);
- with the relevant skills to work with colleagues and parents (48 per cent);
- to establish and maintain a good standard of discipline (59 per cent);

- for teaching pupils of different abilities (59 per cent);
- with the knowledge, skills and understanding to use ICT in their subject teaching (61 per cent).

Many of the issues associated with these aspects of learning to teach have been raised earlier, but working with pupils from minority ethnic groups and with those with English as an additional language (EAL) is discussed in more detail below.

Teaching pupils from ethnic minority backgrounds

In discussing the teaching of pupils from ethnic minority backgrounds many student teachers said they welcomed the opportunity to work in ethnically mixed schools and to learn about cultures of which, in some cases, they had previously known very little. Overall, many commented very favourably on relationships between young people in such schools and those between staff and pupils. Student teachers wanted to make a difference and working in ethnically mixed settings was one way of doing this. Student teachers from ethnic minority back- grounds themselves frequently valued the opportunities to draw on knowledge of their own communities in their work in school. Some spoke of their past experiences of balancing family expectations with those of their peer group. This had given them an understanding of pressures that young people from their community faced and that might be transferable to other communities. However, some also spoke of misplaced assumptions. For example, a teacher from a Sikh back- ground felt that she had been deliberately placed in a school with high numbers of pupils from ethnic minority backgrounds. However, these were children from Moslem backgrounds and she felt a great deal of apprehension in teaching there – though, as she later admitted, her apprehension turned out to be misplaced too.

Many student teachers described how they were insistent that they made no special plans to take account of race and ethnicity in their classroom. At first sight this may seem culturally insensitive but the point they were making was that what worked in their lessons (typi- cally an appropriate level of challenge for each pupil, well-defined routines in class and ongoing assessment and target setting) cut across backgrounds and ability. They were aware of the wider picture of dis- advantage and prejudice that affected some pupils in the school but felt they had to put this to one side. This was expressed by Liz, herself a black teacher:

> If you ask me have I felt direct discrimination in this school I would say no, but it is not as easy as that. You are aware all the time that there is prejudice in society. I am aware of it and I am aware of what some of our pupils experience. But you have to get on with it. I have to put it behind me and so do they if we are going to make the lesson work.

At the same time Liz did look for opportunities for pupils to share experiences and to be positive about diversity in school and wider society. These opportunities existed for teachers in all subjects but were more obvious in some subjects than others; for example, in the work on migration in English and history, or in a discussion of faiths in RE, or in discussions of the nature of citizenship in PSHE. Several student teachers explained how they tried to anticipate cultural issues arising in their teaching; for example, they were aware of how communities were represented in set texts, and they paid attention to the wider community that the school served. They used opportunities to find out more about the school's catchment area and any special events or tensions in the community. Sometimes this paid off in terms of developing relationships with young people, as Jason explains when talking about Muslim festivals:

> I knew nothing about Eid and what it entailed until I came to this school but I made an effort to ask questions and find out. It really helped to understand how pupils were reacting during Ramadan and also how they approached the celebrations afterwards. I could give an example of that. A child who was getting quite high and difficult in my lessons after he came back from celebrating Eid. He said 'Sorry, but you see it is a time when we go off the rails a bit.' I turned round and said 'Yes, but it is also a day of religious significance' and I could explain something of what I understood about the festival. He was startled that I had been interested enough to find this out. It really helped in getting him settled and in building a relationship with him.

The nature of student teachers' concerns in working with children from ethnic minorities differed but there were some general themes.

First, many were worried that they might be seen as culturally insensitive and lacking knowledge of the ethnic minority cultures represented in their schools. Some had understandable concerns that they might misread events in the classroom or be ill equipped to deal with the issues and tensions arising from teaching a particular topic.

Second, for some the teaching of children from ethnic minorities had become unhelpfully blurred with particular concerns in teaching pupils for whom English was an additional language. They were worried that their use of English was pitched at too high a level to make the lesson accessible to all children in the class – something raised most starkly when teaching children of asylum seekers or other new arrivals into the country who very often knew very little English. A further complication here was working with support staff in school, a new experience for many.

A third concern was simply that they had been carrying out their training programme in schools with very few children from ethnic minority backgrounds and felt unprepared for the year ahead. As Juliet explains:

> We had so few pupils from ethnic minority backgrounds that as a group of student teachers we were talking to and observing the same pupils! I don't think we got a very balanced view about the issues and I don't think all the attention was good for those particular pupils.

Your concerns in teaching pupils from ethnic minority groups will be heavily influenced by your own background and experiences. For example, if you are yourself from an ethnic minority strongly represented in the school you may benefit from knowledge of community languages or knowledge of 'street' culture but you may also have concerns with expectations placed on you. But whatever your background your work in the classroom is, again, going to be heavily influenced by the wider context of the school and the community beyond the school. For example, your job is easier if you are carrying out training in a school that involves, and has the confidence of, parents and pupils from all backgrounds. Such a school will have developed and monitored its policies and will have been proactive in explaining its work to you. Better still if the school has been supported by outside agencies and you can get insight into welfare and support services. In contrast, you are almost certainly going to experience tensions in your class if there are poor lines of communication between the school and parents and the wider community. Whatever your circumstances during your placement try to take the opportunities on offer to talk to colleagues who have special responsibilities for working with children from ethnic minorities and seek information on data and attainment. For example, recent figures have pointed to a diversity within pupils from different minority ethnic backgrounds, and particular concerns for pupils from black Caribbean backgrounds. This points to a wide range of factors influencing an individual pupil's attainment. To take two obvious examples, pupils from different minority ethnic groups do not all share EAL issues and pupils who are newly arrived will have very different experiences and expectations to those who were born and raised in this country.

In working with pupils from ethnic minorities the key word is inclusion. As seen earlier this means making your teaching accessible through providing contexts that pupils find relevant and paying close attention to the language used in the classroom. A great deal of help and support is available here – see, for example, Commission for Racial Equality 2000; DfES 2000; OFSTED 1999, 2001. Like Luke, try to demonstrate your interest in other cultures through talking to pupils and showing respect for their background. Children from ethnic minority backgrounds rate the idea of a listening school very highly (Bourne and Blair 1998) as, understandably, they often feel they live in a society in which their cultural traditions are undervalued. This raises a particular challenge in working with newly arrived children, particularly those with very weak language skills and suffering displacement and, in some cases, trauma (Children of the Storm 1998; Allen *et al.* 2004; Rutter 2001). Use your colleagues and specialist support service to help you uncover their background and experiences.

English as an additional language (EAL)

Language issues cut across ethnic background but, as already seen, some student teachers' concerns about teaching pupils from ethnic minorities were focused on those for whom English is an additional language. Here, again, colleagues with special expertise in this area can help you – seek them out. Look at how you can make the language you use as clear as possible and supported by visual clues; for example, use pictures and diagrams to support text in handouts. Look at the reading levels in your material and how you present text – for example, is it well spaced and in an appropriate font? You may need to simplify writing tasks for some pupils: at its most basic this may involve 'match text to picture' exercises, filling in missing words in a text from a list supplied (cloze procedures). At a more advanced level you might prepare sequencing exercises and developing structures for writing – so called writing frames. There are special issues in working with new arrivals to the country who may know very little English. Again, seek help. Useful advice is to aim to be a good language model by speaking slowly, but use a natural voice. Introduce yourself, write down your name for these pupils, make sure they know who you are and encourage them to respond to greetings and goodbyes. You can be easy going about children's use of their first language and make use of those who speak the same language to translate if this is possible. Find ways of encouraging new arrivals to work with other children; for example, by taking turns in practical tasks such as giving out books. Even over a short placement you might notice the progress that new arrivals make in their use of English. However, it will take much longer for pupils to gain mastery of academic writing and you might have pupils whose level of understanding is masked by the difficulties they have with written English. A spin-off in working with pupils with special language difficulties is that it sensitises you to the problems experienced by a great many pupils no matter what their ethnic background.

You might, of course, have very limited opportunities to work with pupils with EAL and/or pupils from ethnic minority groups. Here you will need to be proactive if nothing has been organised in your training programme. Try to arrange an extended visit to another school, perhaps, to work with a colleague from your training programme. Try to find a school that has a good reputation for working with pupils with EAL.

Special educational needs (SEN)

Very similar points can be made about working with pupils with SEN as with EAL, in that the focus is on inclusion or adoption rather than integration in the formal sense of having pupils physically integrated into a lesson (Hartas 2004). This means adjusting your teaching to make your lesson as accessible as possible. You will want to search out specialist support staff and consider carefully policies and procedures in your school. You will also want to make sure you have detailed information on pupils identified as having special needs, and the support in place for them. This will lead you to liaise more closely with the support staff in the classroom. Give them details of your lesson in advance and discuss any suggestions for adapting that lesson.

You might also raise concerns about pupils who are not identified as having SEN, but whose behaviour or progress is causing you considerable concern. Special need is a broad subject and often divided into categories such as learning difficulties, emotional and behavioural difficulties, communication difficulties and physical difficulties, although some of these may well overlap.

Support staff can talk you through different strategies for addressing individual special needs. Once described these often appear as common sense, for example wait until you have eye contact before you start speaking to a pupil with hearing difficulties, but nonetheless they still need pointing out. Of course, many of the challenges you face are going to be persistent and fairly intractable in the short term. For example, you may find a child with emotional difficulties who has come to rely on his or her existing class teacher for emotional and practical support and still resents your presence. Here, you will need to discuss strategies for working with this pupil with support staff and the class teacher concerned.

Working with pupils with special needs may have important spin-offs for your teaching in general. For example, you know that a pupil with a particular learning difficulty will not understand you if you do not speak clearly, use visual aids and highlight key words. If you can address these needs then not only will the individual pupil benefit but so will the whole class. A guide to organisations that support pupils with special needs is given in Appendix D.

Office for Standards in Education (OFSTED)

Between 1999 and 2002 OFSTED inspected all 600 courses offered by training providers, covering 16 subjects in total. Part of the inspection process involved the observation of a representative sample of student teachers within each course. An overview report on secondary initial teacher training (OFSTED 2003) praised the quality of training inspectors had seen as good, much of it very good. With respect to lesson observations, half of students' lessons were described as good or very good. Only one in ten lessons was less than satisfactory in some respects and there were very few poor lessons. Nine out of ten student teachers showed good knowledge and understanding of their subject. Four out of five student teachers planned their teaching well. Classes were well managed. The report concluded that today's newly qualified teachers are 'the best trained that we have ever had'. This is the kind of reporting that will make you feel confident about the year ahead.

However, not everything is rosy. OFSTED raised concerns over exclusively school-based routes and variation between different subjects. They also noted that the behaviour of pupils in some schools affected some student teachers. There were gaps in training in behaviour management and some student teachers had limited strategies for dealing with disruptive pupils. OFSTED also found poor provision for ICT in many subject departments and reduced opportunities for some student teachers to use ICT.

In addition to worries over teaching at post-16 level, the report raised general concerns over assessment. Student teachers were said to lack focus on specific learning objectives and there were gaps in the use of formative feedback, record keeping, and some had not had the experience of reporting to parents.

Knowing your class

There is a great deal of overlap between the TTA survey, OFSTED's review of teacher training and, indeed, wider research into learning to teach. There are some differences too, but behind some of these differences, for example NQTs' concern over the progression of individual pupils and OFSTED's concern over assessment, perhaps there is a common thread. As a student teacher you are aware that a class is made up of individuals with their own starting points, different backgrounds, interests and rates of progress and their own preferred learning styles, but perhaps your knowledge of each individual pupil is limited. Broadly speaking it seems that most student teachers learn the 'teaching' side of the job very well – they have presence in the class, they plan their work, they explain the topic they are covering, they organise pupils, they set targets, they learn to maintain order, they report back on what has been done and so on. However, what might be called the 'learning' side of the job, knowledge of each pupil and how best to manage their learning, takes longer. This is not in the least surprising. In learning to teach you are trying to manage your teaching and monitor pupils' learning at the same time. To develop an earlier analogy, it is rather like being an actor who has to learn all their lines and stage movements but, every so often, join the audience and find out what they make of the show so far and adapt accordingly. Of course, your audience does not fill a theatre but there may be 30 or more individuals in your class and if you divided your time equally you would barely have more than a minute a lesson with each child. There are gaps in what you know and perhaps this comes home to you when there are pupils with special needs or pupils from different cultures to your own. With more experience, teachers do get to know their pupils better and are better able to pick up patterns in the ways pupils think about and learn a subject. You can prepare for this within your training programme by focusing on particular pupils in your class; for example, you can monitor their learning within a lesson and become more involved in tutor group activities and PSHE lessons. You can look again at the data you have on pupils and, in particular, those identified with special needs. Talk to those with most knowledge of your pupils, heads of year, SEN coordinators – and try to get a wider picture of their lives.

For you to do

Try to organise a series of lessons in which you are teaching only a small group of pupils. Talk to the individuals within the group, observe the way they work together and the work they produce. Can you accurately describe what each knows about a topic before you teach them and can you identify any preferred learning styles? Draw conclusions as to what each individual pupil has learnt, what has triggered that learning and what has been holding them back. Discuss the implications of this small-group work for your whole-class teaching with your mentor and other colleagues.

Summary

This chapter has looked at:

- strengths in your teaching;
- areas to develop;
- surveys into training programme;
- knowing your pupils.

A key message is to look for opportunities to know more about your pupils and how they learn your subject.

Chapter 3

Becoming a better teacher

The previous two chapters have described some of the ways in which your views of teaching may have changed and identified strengths and areas to develop in your teaching. This chapter continues by looking in greater depth at the strategies open to you to develop your teaching. It will help you:

- identify strategies for developing your teaching;
- consider the value of targets and target setting;
- use your career entry and development profile.

Strategies to develop your teaching

Teacher development is often thought of as something that happens to you rather than something that you make happen. This is not surprising given how much you learn through experience. However, from day one of your training you are taking an active part in your development by watching, listening and talking to teachers, by reading about teaching and by planning your lessons, by trying things out and getting feedback on what has happened. As your placement has progressed you will have found valuable insight into your teaching through evaluation, being observed and learning from others.

Evaluating your own teaching

Your own analysis of your teaching is critical in your development as a teacher and you may well feel you are making pretty accurate judgements on how your classes have gone. Analysing your teaching invariably involves stepping back and trying to see the lesson from the viewpoint of the pupils. Here, Tom, an English teacher, explains how this helped him see where his lesson hit the rails:

Half way through the class I could see that they did not know they should be writing the piece from the view point of the boy in the story. They were not being silly, it was me. I had given them different possibilities in the introduction, I wasn't clear enough. Fortunately they got on with it the best they could and I could talk to them about it later, but next time I need to set out the instructions clearly.

This was an honest appraisal in which Tom did not dwell on his mistake but, instead, set out to learn from it and change his approach to giving instructions in a following lesson. A more sophisticated approach to lesson evaluation is taken here by Yvette, a teacher of modern foreign languages, who considered pupils' preferred learning styles in reaching judgements of her teaching:

At the start I had a fairly one track view on what I was going to give pupils but I could see it didn't always work. Now I am much more aware of the things that appeal to different people and I try to bring this into my evaluations. I can see if you are someone who likes oral work much more than writing then I know some of my lessons miss the mark. But others are terrified of speaking so they will see the same lesson in a different way.

Yvette went beyond thinking about what *a* learner would make of the lesson to thinking how different types of learner would respond; for example, what if it was someone who liked talking and role play? What if they did not like writing? What if they had difficulties in listening? Questions like these provided a major focus for her evaluation and fed into her planning of follow-up lessons.

Self-reflection is the most accessible, and hence the most valuable, tool you have to develop your teaching especially when you go on to make changes in your teaching in the light of experience. However, you face difficulties if left to your own devices. For example, many student teachers are overly critical of themselves. As one student teacher said: 'If you have done something wrong you tend to see it straight away, you have to do something right ten times before you can recognise it as a strength.' Others can be very superficial in their evaluation of lessons and many are, not surprisingly, too focused on their role in the classroom rather than their planning and assessment of pupils. For this reason it is useful to consider the evidence of pupils' learning when reaching judgements on your own teaching. In the first instance this means monitoring pupils: what have they been doing and why have they achieved or not achieved? This is something you probably now do routinely. For example, you engage in question and answer activities with the whole class and with individuals in the class, you examine pupils' work and develop plenary activities with formal and informal feedback.

Some teachers go further and seek pupil feedback on their work and on the kinds of activity they find useful in helping them learn. For example, Janet, a science teacher, designed a short questionnaire asking pupils to rank in order of preference the activities they had done, what they had found most difficult and what had helped them most in understanding the topic:

> Looking back it could have backfired, giving them a chance to say what a lousy teacher I was, but most did it sensibly. Of course, I had a pretty good idea as to what they had understood and what they liked doing, but I hadn't realised how little they had got from the experimental work. I had assumed they liked this bit of the unit but they did not as much as I had thought and it was clear that many did not know what they were supposed to get out of it. I need to build in the discussion part much more – it was all a bit of an eye opener really.

Your own evaluation of lessons is important, along with pupil feedback, but you will still want to set your own judgements against those of other professionals.

Observation of lessons

Most student teachers value tutor and mentor feedback on their teaching very highly and the vast majority are very receptive to having people watch their lessons. Feedback is helpful on both the emotional and practical level. Here, Marie tells how she appreciated the positive tone adopted by her mentor:

> I honestly felt I was a hopeless case after the lesson. If he had ripped me apart I would have given up then and there. But he instinctively knew how much I could handle and found some things to praise about the lesson and found words of encouragement – it meant loads to me.

Eddie found his mentor's comments were essential in developing his planning:

> I felt quite nervous about being watched but it turned out to be very useful. I think I was worried about seeing her going round and the children saying it was boring or they didn't understand. It's so easy if you're watching to focus on the child not working and say to the teacher you've missed this or missed that. Anyway it went all right and she did point out those who were struggling but rather than pick me up on it together we thought about how I could give all the pupils a starting point for next lesson.

Derek found feedback from his professional mentor equally important in helping him focus on classroom management. In his case he had agreed to have the beginning of his lesson video recorded using a simple hand-held machine focused on him:

> Later we looked at the video tapes together. It was an eye opener to see how long it took for the lesson to get started, the register, the interruptions, the getting settled and one really cringing bit when I got their attention and then got muddled in what I wanted to tell them. But it was very useful as she could show me just how long I was taking to do the routine stuff like doing the register or giving out the starter activity and just how rushed I was when I had something to say. I'd go, 'Right listen, I'm waiting for quiet', and launch into the start of the lesson. She explained that a more experienced teacher would use the quiet – hold them for a few seconds, remind them of the importance of listening and then get them back. We also picked out moments in the introduction when I could alter my voice – so it was not all at the same level.

Some, like Carlton also benefited from feedback from their fellow students:

> The best part of the course was working with each other. We would share resources and keep in touch with the ones you got on with. And when one of my mates observed me, he could be much more open about it, you knew it was coming from someone who knew what you were going through.

Observing other teachers

Training programmes differ in structure and in levels of commitment and support. Not surprisingly, student teachers often say they are most influenced by people who have provided them with engaging models of teaching and practical insight into dealing with the classes they are going to teach. Colin, for example, found his university tutor inspiring:

> The biggest influence on me as someone learning to teach is Sue (the university tutor). It is about how she sets up the class, you want to be there, she makes sure you know everyone and work with everyone. There is a lot of variety in what you do. She encourages everyone to participate and will look out for those not offering ideas and ask them directly, 'What would you think?' So there are good ideas which get shared around, ideas for working in class. She makes sure she brings it down to your level, she doesn't say, 'Do it like this' but she'll go, 'Look, this is my idea for teaching this topic but you are teaching this to a class of Y9s, what would you do?' and then give you feedback of her own.

Here, Colin is describing the value of a collaborative environment in which he can share ideas with other students. He is looking for a focus on the practical issues he faces. The teacher offers him a problem-solving approach posing possible scenarios and asking 'What would you do in this situation?' Colin highlights the different roles which the tutor takes: someone who is attentive to the social relationships in the class, who uses creative questions to encourage students to articulate their own ideas but who is equally capable of taking a more directed role, telling or showing ideas of her own. This not only provides Colin with what has been called a 'powerful learning environment' (de Corte *et al.* 2003) but gives him a model of the kind of classroom he would like to create in school. Another student teacher, Stephen, explains how he was inspired by a teacher in his placement school. Through working with this teacher he came to see the importance of making learning more clearly relevant:

> The biggest influence on me in this school has been Zoe. I have been teaching her Y8s. She is really a PE teacher who teaches a bit of geography to help out. I thought at first, 'Oh no I want to see a subject specialist', but she is just so good at thinking up ideas for involving pupils that I was taken aback. Sometimes simple ideas like getting them to imagine themselves in the role

of a journalist investigating an environmental disaster. All the time she is pushing me to think how we can make it appeal to them.

Student teachers often draw attention to how much they learnt not simply from an individual teacher but, like Sukbir, by being in a department with more experienced teachers willing to talk about their work:

> I learnt a lot just by asking questions, 'how do you do that?', 'what do you think if I did this?' and sometimes just watching how they would talk to the kids. I was lucky, you could always go up to someone and say 'I don't know how to do this' and they would show you or tell you how they did it. Comparing notes I was lucky to find myself working where there was such a sense of all being in it together.

Learning inside a department becomes much easier if you have tutors, mentors and departmental colleagues who all share a similar philosophy. Many student teachers explained how this became very important in considering assessment practices in school – an area of concern within many training programmes. Here, recent research has emphasised the importance of formative assessment, assessment for learning (see Box 3.1), as well as assessment of learning. Mark explains how the principles behind formative assessment came alive through working in his department:

> In our school we were being constantly told that the point of assessment was to help pupils recognise their strengths and look at how they can improve. This principle lay behind everything we did, the way we talked to them in class, the comments we made, the end of lesson plenaries, the whole thing. There was a lot of emphasis on collection of evidence in portfolios, most of the pupils were really proud of their work and we could look back at their progress over the year. This made it easier for us to have something to base our end of year assessments on.

Like Carlton, earlier, Barbara found it useful to work with another student teacher but this time to observe a lesson in another school:

> All through the course I got very close to Julie. We just hit it off. I learnt so much by seeing her in school. All the time you are seeing people who seem to know what they are doing, but

Box 3.1 Advice on assessment for learning

There is a lot of advice on assessment in the key stage 3 strategy (DfES 2002a), much of which has been influenced by work by Black and Wiliam (1998). Key ideas, illustrated within the strategy documents are to:

- share learning objectives with pupils and doing so in a pupil friendly language;
- involve pupils in peer- and self-assessment;
- give pupils opportunities to talk about what they have learnt, and what they have found difficult and to identify where they still have difficulties;
- provide feedback that leads to pupils recognising their next steps and how to take them;
- involve both teacher and pupils in reviewing and reflecting on assessment information, what pupils have learnt and understood, and providing oral as well as written feedback whenever possible;
- encouraging pupils to explain their thinking and reasoning.

There are considerable spin-offs for teachers as well as pupils in developing assessment practice. You become much more aware of pupils' misconceptions and difficulties and better able to adapt your teaching in the future. Assessment can inform planning rather than being seen as something tacked on to the end of a lesson or scheme of work almost as an an afterthought.

While few people would argue against developing formative assessment there are constraints on what you can achieve. There is the problem of time. In many classrooms teachers do not have the time to engage in detailed discussion with pupils. There are ways around this – chiefly self-assessment and whole-class discussion – but both of these require considerable planning and modelling. It is made much easier if there is a whole-school policy on 'thinking skills' (learning how to learn) so that goal setting and reflection become second nature. The problem here is that most schools are rarely successful at implementing cross-curricular strategies. A message once again is to go for small, sustainable changes in assessment of your pupils.

sometimes you need to see all the joins, to see where things go wrong and why they go wrong. Don't get me wrong, Julie is a good teacher, I can see it, but you need sometimes to sit there and see it in slow motion almost.

Learning from others: using resources

Whatever your training programme, you will have been introduced to a wide range of material giving you the opportunity to learn from others, albeit from a distance. For example, you will have been provided with access to the general literature on preparing to teach (e.g. Capel *et al*. 1995; Dillon *et al*. 2001; Brooks *et al*. 2004; Marland 2002) and an extensive list of subject-specific support material too wide to list here. You might find your attitude to these resources changing as you have more experience. Some may provide a clearer guide to action now you can see the advice in the context of the pupils in your particular classroom. In contrast, experience may have only confirmed your view of the inappropriate nature of some of the material. Often, like Alice, student teachers talk about the value of the literature for orientation to a problem rather than pointing to simple solutions for the classroom:

> I look back on the readings and it is hard to say I have used this or that but it has made me aware of the bigger picture, for example ideas about differentiation in the classroom and why it is important. But no one can really provide me with the nuts and bolts on what I should do with these children.

A significant feature of many training programmes has been a focus on DfES-supported curriculum advice, including teaching support documents and videos. Here the key stage 3 strategy documents, covering literacy, numeracy, foundation and non-foundation subjects have been important (see glossary of key terms in Appendix B for more details). A closely related set of materials, 'Teaching and Learning in Secondary Schools' with added video support, is available in a set of twenty units (reference to two of these units has already been made: DfES 2003b, 2003c). While generating controversy and debate, the key stage 3 strategy has been enormously influential on practice in schools within and beyond the 11–14 curriculum. In comparison with more general literature the strategy material is more practical and more prescriptive, and the video support adds considerable value. However, the material does not provide an 'off the peg' solution to teaching and learning but, rather, works best when it offers ideas for addressing your concerns, which you can adapt to meet your needs. Jonathon, a business studies teacher, explains his experience with the literacy strategy support for writing (DfES 2001):

> Oddly enough the literacy strategy has had a big impact on the way I think about getting children to write. I say oddly because I don't think many in my group were that bothered about the material but I found I could get on with it. I could see that it gives you a model to work from when you want the class to do some writing. I think left to myself I would have said write this or write that, keep it very free and open, but here you are being asked to demonstrate what their writing should look like and give them pointers to help them get there. Bits (of the advice) are over the top, I couldn't discuss writing at the level they want me to or I would lose the children. I have no idea what my English teaching colleagues make of it. It is not exactly creative writing, but the way the strategy sets it out has helped me as a business studies teacher and I have a model to use even if I don't always want to use it.

Jonathon found the model within the strategy (in which teachers were encouraged to provide, and explain features of, texts, and to guide pupils in joint composition, before carrying out independent writing of their own) helped him work with his pupils. His first attempts at using the model had been too complex but he adapted them in the light of experience.

A further source of 'official' material on teaching and learning is available from OFSTED and you will almost certainly have seen OFSTED commentaries on teaching your subject (if not go to the web address given in Appendix C). OFSTED material is often more broad brush, alerting you to strengths and difficulties in teaching and learning rather than providing you with fine-tuned curriculum advice.

You will have your own views on the value of the resources you have seen during your programme. No one has a blueprint for how you should teach. Other people are most influential when they tell you or show you things that seem to chime with your own ideas about teaching and which make sense in teaching your particular classes. But you will want to adapt these ideas and make them your own.

Focus questions

- What or who has helped you most in learning to teach?
- How can you take further advantage of this person or this resource before the end of your training programme?
- Reflect on the evaluations you make on your teaching. How can they become more focused on pupils' learning? Use a recent lesson evaluation to identify something you might change if teaching the lesson again.

Target setting for professional learning

The previous chapter presented examples of teachers setting targets for developing their teaching. Whatever the pros and cons of defining learning to teach against certain standards there is no doubt about the usefulness of setting explicit goals for developing your teaching. In many cases these have been described as SMART targets (Specific, Measurable, Achievable, Realistic and Time-related), an approach which, while simplistic, is undoubtedly useful in focusing attention. There is a simple point. Developing your teaching involves setting goals and paying attention to whether or not you achieve them. Much will depend on a sympathetic and insightful mentor. For example, Samantha found it natural to focus on targets arising directly from an observation of her teaching:

> One of things I was aware of was that I could not get whole-class discussion going at the start of the lesson. It was the same one or two hands that would go up and I quickly moved on to getting them working by themselves. I was not happy with this and talked it over with my mentor. He suggested that one thing he had found useful was having them working in pairs before answering. I thought that this would be unmanageable and they would go off task but he said he would show me the next lesson. So he came into the class and said, 'Right, turn to the person you are sitting next to, you have two minutes to come up with three things you learnt last lesson.' They got on with it and all had something to say when he did the whole-class bit and asked them about the topic. The thing is they did not have time to worry

about working together, they just did it. So he said to me, 'Right, you finish the lesson in a similar way.' I gave them two minutes to write down with a partner the three most important things they had learnt and then we all talked about it. He watched this part of the lesson and said it was fine but told me I was fussing around them too much and gave them more than two minutes. This was useful to hear. I felt I have grown as a teacher. I don't have to use pair work all the time but I have something in the locker, I can use when it seems right.

Like Samantha you may find that a target works when you have identified for yourself an area of concern. Discussion with your mentor gives you an opportunity to articulate your concerns and to listen to advice on dealing with them. In many cases you are looking to be shown a new way of working that will help and that you can put into practice. You will then want immediate feedback on how you got on (Figure 3.1).

As so much depends on the relationship you have with your mentor the obvious advice here is to choose your mentor carefully. In reality, you might have had very little input into where you carry out your training and you might view it as your good fortune that you are receiving the help and support you need. You might not be so fortunate and, notwithstanding quality control procedures in place in your institution, you might be experiencing difficulties in working with your mentor. Sometimes these are personal: you do not seem to hit it off with your mentor or perhaps their prevailing style of teaching is not one in which you feel comfortable. Very few student teachers question the good intentions and willingness of tutors or mentors in school, but not everyone has experience of good-quality modelling and coaching. Even at this late stage in your training programme try to address any concerns you may have – obviously it helps to do this in a positive way. For example, saying 'I would find it helpful if you could demonstrate this to me with my class' will be more productive than going over past difficulties. Be realistic about what you can expect: your mentor will be overstretched but will also have a specific responsibility for supporting you. Look again at the full range of support in the school. Try to identify ways in which you can compensate for the shortcomings in your mentoring. You will know the department much better by now, ask teachers in your department you have learnt to trust to allow you to carry out further observations of their teaching. Ask for further support from your professional mentor and ask to see expert practitioners in other departments. If appropriate to your programme ask for further support from your university tutors. Organise peer visits with colleagues in other schools. Try to use the remaining time within your placement to push your teaching on, rather than see the last days or weeks as ones to get through.

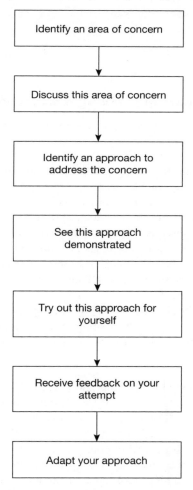

Figure 3.1 Using target setting to develop your teaching

For you to do

Look back at the areas for development you identified in the previous chapter. Ask for an observation on your teaching and feedback on how well you are meeting your targets for development. Try to identify other support for your teaching within your school.

Support for teaching: taking a wider view

There are, then, opportunities for developing your teaching in and beyond the classroom:

- in the classroom: for example, what you learn by planning, teaching and assessing pupils' learning, through reflection on your teaching and through direct pupil feedback;
- in your department: for example, through observation of your teaching and observing other teachers of your subject, by team teaching, by talking to colleagues in formal and informal settings;
- in your school: for example, by observing teachers and student teachers of other subjects; by talking to colleagues in formal and informal settings;
- beyond the school: for example, by visiting and observing student teachers in other schools; visiting other schools and attending training events; visits of tutors, reading and viewing curriculum material.

Almost inevitably your thinking about teaching will be dominated by the classroom and the day-to-day planning, teaching and assessing of the classes for which you have responsibility. However, try not to let the immediate needs of the classroom eclipse other types of support. As you reach the end of your placement try to 'get out more', both literally and metaphorically. Look for opportunities to get wider feedback on your teaching; look again at the more general curriculum advice; and try to get a picture of the way the whole school works. One very practical means of doing this is pupil tracking as discussed below.

Pupil tracking

During the course of your training programme you will have observed many lessons. For obvious reasons this usually happens at the start of your training rather than at the end. This is a great pity because you can see more and you are more aware of what is going on when you have more experience of teaching. Towards the end of the academic year, when timetables are sometimes freed up a little with examination leave, you may have more opportunities to carry out extended observations into teaching, more in the nature of curriculum inquiry than familiarisation with the classes you are going to teach. One approach you might take towards the end of your time in school is to revisit pupil tracking.

Put briefly, pupil tracking means following a pupil or set or class of pupils through more than one lesson, typically over a half or full day. Pupil tracking can extend into break and lunch times. The most important reason to track pupils is to give you insight into the markedly different ways in which individual pupils respond to different teachers and subjects. Pupils are not simply 'like this or that'; to some extent at least, how they behave and what they learn depends on the circumstances in which they find themselves. You will also find that tracking gives you a sense of the rhythm of the day, the low and high points as experienced by the pupils, and it gives you a perspective on the prevailing culture of the school. You will be able to describe the balance of activities that pupils engage in, e.g. do they spend most of the day talking, reading, working individually, how many questions does an individual pupil ask a teacher during the day, how many opportunities do pupils have to share work with their peers?

You might recall observations of lessons less than fondly from your earlier experience in school. You might feel like an intruder, or, as more than one student teacher put it, ' a spare part'. Your presence in class might embarrass teachers and create tensions. You might find events in the lesson unfolding too quickly and feel unable to process the questions teachers are asking. You might feel unable to account for the pupil behaviour you are witnessing. However, you can plan to make tracking a useful exercise.

Identify which pupils are most appropriate for you to track. You will want to consider the age range, the span of lessons on a particular day and to check if there are any special events like exams or school trips that will affect your plans. You might offer to track the tutor group to which you are attached. This gives you more opportunity to explain your role to pupils, to check your previous assumptions about the pupils, and to follow up what you learnt with pupils. Explain to pupils what you are doing and why you are doing it. If you would like to track individuals during break and lunch times discuss this with pupils and your mentor. Talk to the teachers whose classes you are observing and check arrangements such as where you are going to sit and if it is alright to carry out interviews with pupils. Point out that you are not judging their performance as a teacher. Again, the process may already be quite familiar to them but you cannot take this for granted. You might want to ask the teacher to explain your presence to the class at the start of the lesson.

You will need to plan in advance what you want to observe and how you are going to record your observations. There are many different foci for your observations but most of them gravitate towards teachers and their teaching and pupils and their learning – though, of course, observations about teaching are also ones about learning.

Teachers and teaching

You might want to focus on how individual teachers work with the class. Tracking the pupils for the whole day will give you opportunities to compare and contrast teachers. For example, you might have a particular concern with, say, questioning or differentiation in which case you could use your tracking of the pupils to observe the ways in which teachers approach these aspects of their teaching and the varying response of pupils.

Pupils and pupil learning

You might want to focus on how individual pupils or groups of pupils work or the kinds of learning activities with which they are expected to engage. You can use the day to compare and contrast the way they respond to different teachers and subjects. For example, you might have particular knowledge of a pupil, you think that they respond well to group work but badly to writing exercises. Is this borne out over the day? Similarly, you may have become aware of pupils with special needs in the school through your teaching and through working with your school's special needs coordinator. You may want to track how different teachers respond to these particular pupils.

Organising your observations of lessons

Having decided the focus for your observations you will want to design an appropriate schedule. For example, if you are interested in teacher questioning you will want to record different types of question, perhaps using Bloom's taxonomy (Bloom 1956) which differentiates between lower order questions, requiring recall and application, and higher order ones, assessing pupils' grasp of analysis, synthesis and evaluation. You are not going to get your schedule right first time so test it out through a one-off observation before you do a longer tracking exercise. The key questions are: are you recording appropriate data and is the recording manageable? You will not get a schedule that covers everything, be prepared to refine it.

During the day

Incidents will go quickly and you could benefit enormously by video taping parts of the lesson (a small hand-held machine is fine for your purposes) and playing this back later. Alternatively, record on audio tape some of the conversations you had with pupils or teachers. However, you must check out the ethical issues in advance, at the very least teachers will want notice and a set of guidelines about when and where any tape can be used. Most would probably rather you did not film.

Make sure you have completed relevant notes at the end of each lesson and reflect on what you have seen: you might want to make alterations to your pro forma for the following lessons.

You will have to decide how closely you want to become involved with the group; for example, if you are tracking the same set of pupils you would naturally want to ask them about their day and their learning. You cannot plan for every eventuality but design an interview schedule to help you identify in advance the questions you would like to ask. As you do this think through the ethical and professional issues. For example, asking a pupil what aspects of learning geography they like is acceptable but 'Do you like your geography teacher?' is not.

If at all possible discuss the lessons you observe with the teachers. They might feel vulnerable if the lesson did not go as well as they had hoped but find something positive to say before asking further questions.

After the event

Your job is to analyse your data and put it to good use in your teaching. You can do this by focusing on general impressions; analysing your observation data; and considering the consequences for your teaching.

General impressions

These are useful for organising your thoughts and identifying important findings that lie beyond your focused inquiry. For example, you might want to ask yourself:

* How would I feel if I was a pupil going to experience a similar day tomorrow?
* What really impressed me about teaching and learning over the day?
* What really surprised me?
* What kind of teaching inspired me?
* What would I, as a teacher, try to avoid?
* What does this school do really well?

Focused observations

Here, you will want to aggregate and analyse the data you have recorded. For example, you might want to provide a quantitative break-down of teacher and pupil activity over the day. You might find, for example, pupils spent much longer than you thought they would getting settled, that they spent more time writing than listening and reading or that group work was far less prevalent than you anticipated. Supplied with the data you might then want to look at what was common to the classes you saw. For example, why did most classes take so long to settle? What kind of writing was asked of pupils and why did some find this so difficult? Were most of the questions teachers asked lower order ones and why might this be the case? But also look at the teachers who diverged from the norm. How was it teacher A got their class settled much earlier than other teachers? Why was teacher B alone in using structured group work and what were the consequences here for pupils' learning? If teachers spent most of their time asking lower order questions, recall and analyse what happened when teachers asked higher order questions.

In addition to aggregating data you could review your notes and look at critical incidents. For example, if you have been tracking a particular child what triggered them to go off/go back on task, did those triggers work in the same way across different subjects and which teachers avoided those triggers and did they successfully avoid confrontation?

Discuss what you have seen with a fellow student carrying out a similar analysis, or with your mentor.

Drawing conclusions for your teaching

In this phase use your analysis to identify goals for your own teaching. Consider the evidence that has led you to these aspirations and the action you are going to take. Some examples are given in Box 3.2.

Box 3.2 Identifying goals for your teaching

I aspire to	Evidence from tracking	Action
Be more directed in my use of pair work	Pupils responded by being more task focused and used more productive talk	Plan for short directed tasks
Use more variety in my teaching	Pupils spent most of the day reading and writing and many were bored	Plan for kinaesthetic activity, e.g. role play (discuss support needed for this)
Use a wider range of questions with pupils	Teachers asked a very restricted range of questions but higher order questions were triggers for pupils' thinking	Script questions for the start of each lesson
Use silence to encourage pupils to settle	Pupils responded negatively to overly confrontational teachers	Aide mémoire for lesson plan: stay calm, wait

Through this kind of analysis you may well be able to identify targets to develop your teaching based on detailed evidence and what you have seen modelled successfully in the classroom.

Pupil tracking is one route into curriculum inquiry. There are many guides to help you carry out small-scale research of your own. (See, for example, a set put together by the Scottish Research in Education Centre: Drever 2003; Lewis and Munn 2004; Simpson and Tuson 2003; Munn and Drever 1999.)

Career entry and development profiles

In many countries it is common for new teachers to come to a new school with an 'entry profile' of some sort. In England the profile is a record of your strengths and areas for development which provides an orientation to your training programme in your new school. Four focus questions are asked in the present Career Entry and Development Profile (CEPD). These are:

- Which aspect(s) of teaching do you find most interesting and rewarding?
- What do you consider to be your main strengths and achievements as a teacher?
- In which aspects of teaching would you value further experience in the future?
- Do you have any thoughts about how you would like to see your career develop? (TTA 2003c).

Your training provider will provide you with more details about completing this profile but you should have little difficulty in addressing the first three questions if you have followed the focus questions and activities in this first part of the book. The fourth will become much clearer as you read the chapters that follow. Examples of responses to all four questions are provided in Box 3.3.

In an ideal world these profiles give you an opportunity to celebrate your achievements with a valued colleague and to reflect on strategies to make a successful start to your new career. For example, Chris explains:

> The process seemed a bit like a signing off with my tutor. I was really pleased that he had come in and seen me over the course of the year and he knew how much I had come on as a teacher.

Box 3.3 Completing your CEPD: an example

These are examples of comments made by Claire in completing her profile: the italicised focus questions are taken from the original CEPD document (TTA 2003a). Your profile will give you an opportunity to articulate your strengths and areas to develop.

Which aspect(s) of teaching do you find most interesting and rewarding?

- I found working with pupils with EAL most interesting and rewarding. I felt that I developed strategies which made the curriculum accessible to these pupils and working with EAL specialists unlocked the importance of writing frames for me.
- I enjoyed teaching my subject at all key stages and I liked the variety of teaching in an 11–19 school. I found post-16 work very rewarding as it pushed me to develop my subject knowledge.
- I liked innovating within my teaching and found I could plan structured group work activities which engaged pupils and motivated some pupils who had not participated very much in other lessons.
- My achievement is that I know I can teach. I feel confident that with the right support in my new school I can make a good start to my career.

In which aspects of teaching would you value further experience in the future?

- I worked very hard at classroom management during my placement and increased in confidence. I would like to develop more positive approaches to managing children and would like to observe and get feedback from teachers in my new school.
- Despite being attached to a tutor group I feel I have been protected from pastoral responsibility. I do not want a tutor group next year but I want to get a full introduction to tutorial arrangements and to be attached to an experienced classroom tutor who can model good practices for me.

- I would like to work on understanding pupil misconceptions – as a start use questioning effectively to appreciate 'where they are coming from'.
- My post-16 teaching – there are different qualification routes and different exam boards which will leave gaps in my subject knowledge.

Do you have any thoughts about how you would like to see your career develop?
- I am sure I made the right choice to go into teaching. I would like to get further experience of teaching all key stages in my first two or three years in a new school and develop as a confident and skilled all-round teacher. I would like to take on responsibility in a phased way. For example, I could see myself taking on responsibility for introducing vocational options at post-16 once settled into the department.

He kept prompting me to say what I was doing well – I don't find that particularly easy but it was a real confidence boost. This made it much easier to talk about what I had missed in terms of my knowledge – basically vocational courses which I was going to teach next year. I highlighted this on my profile and talked about it at the new school when I visited them. They saw some training as a priority for me, I was given a run-through of the programmes they were offering and saw that I would be supported in my teaching; this will mean regularly sharing notes with the course leader.

The CEPD, like many innovations in education, is undoubtedly a good idea but experience of completing these profiles can be mixed and limited use is made of them in some schools (Totterdell *et al.* 2002). Where CEPD interviews did not work well the process was hurried and bureaucratic and new teachers later found little that was followed up in school. For Jermaine the whole process was a waste of time:

On my last week of the course I had to prepare a list of my strengths and weakness all listed against the standards. The mentor seemed more concerned that I had written something and that it was all 'standard related' as he put it than anything else. The document was sent on to school where I don't think anyone looked at it until the end of my first year. I mean what was the point of it all?

Again, the value of a training event is to some extent out of your hands, but not totally. Use the focus questions within the CEPD – they are sensible ones for anyone to ask at the end of a period of training – to acknowledge your strengths and orient yourself to the next year's teaching. Try to be proactive in stating your training needs.

For you to do

Use your entry profile to articulate your strengths and areas for development. Highlight your support and development needs for next year.

Summary

This chapter has looked at:

*   opportunities for developing your teaching in the classroom, department, school and beyond;
*   target setting;
*   getting a wider view of teaching;
*   the CEPD process.

A key message is to use all the opportunities open to you to develop your teaching, rather than see out the remaining time in school.

Part II

Your first two years in school

Chapter 4

Settling into your first year of teaching

You have come through your training year vastly more skilled and more knowledgeable about teaching. Your motivation remains intact even if you have taken some knocks along the way. You are aware of your strengths but know there are several areas to work on. This chapter takes you through your first year of teaching. This could be a year to look back on with a sense of achievement, the next step on the way to becoming a confident and expert teacher. Alternatively, an unhappy first year might cloud your attitude to teaching, dent your confidence and self-esteem and lead you to look for a way out of the profession.

Everyone will experience the year in different ways. The challenge will look different if this is your first 'proper' job rather than if you are moving into teaching after a previous career. Settling in will look more manageable if you are comfortable with your new timetable, with the school ethos and if you know the local area and the mix of children at the school. But, wherever you start from, you face some common concerns. This chapter will help you:

- prepare in advance of the first term;
- focus on the satisfaction of teaching;
- identify some potential difficulties;
- consider approaches to dealing with stress.

Preparing in advance of the first term

The more you can find out about your new school the better. This will be less of a concern if you are going back to where you carried out a placement, but be aware that the school will look very different when you start in September because you will now be seen as a qualified teacher. Schools differ in the amount of guidance they offer you in advance of the new term. Some schools still leave arrangements very much up to you and your head of department, but others will provide a programme, often managed by an induction tutor and your head of department (HoD).

Your induction tutor will take you through the administrative details: the times of the school day, when you are expected to arrive in the morning, what you should do if sick, when the school is open during the holidays, the pattern of school meetings, access to photo-copying and secretarial support, access to ICT and special equipment or teaching rooms, dress codes for pupils, discipline procedures and so on. Much of this information is contained in the school handbook and the school prospectus. Pay attention to the details because what might be usual practice in your placement school may be considered unacceptable in your new school or vice versa. Some induction tutors will organise a tour around the catchment area and a visit to a feeder school or, where appropriate, the local college of further education or sixth form college.

Your induction tutor will discuss opportunities for professional development, including your mentoring arrangements for next year, his or her responsibilities to you and those of your HoD and head-teacher. He or she will explain the pattern of mentor meetings, arrangements for observations and any inspection of lesson plans. Your tutor will go on to point out opportunities for in-service training organised both inside and outside the school and explain your entitlements to training and support. There may be opportunities to discuss reports on your teaching in advance of the school year and how you can exploit your special strengths or how you have identified areas for development. In particular, you might discuss any areas for development you can address before the start of next term.

Your induction tutor will also take you through or, better, introduce you to those with special responsibilities for, whole-school teaching and learning issues. Topics will include details of pastoral support and you will be given an opportunity to discuss your role in a pastoral team. There may be particular policies and arrangements for SEN and EAL support and policies on bullying and racial abuse to discuss.

From your HoD you will want, above all, to see your timetable for next year and the schemes of work and examination syllabuses towards which you are expected to work. Where available, you will want class lists with relevant data on each pupil, in particular statements on pupils with special needs and the support they are offered. You will want time to work through any teaching resources, to read departmental policy documents and to meet other members of the department, in particular those with special responsibilities such as key stage coordinators, and coordinators of ICT, EAL and SEN within the department. You might find an NQT already working in the department who might be a source of advice. Again, seek opportunities to discuss training and support.

Looking at the list of what you need to know it is not difficult to see why it is increasingly common for schools to invite new teachers to do a couple of weeks of supply teaching in the period between the end of a PGCE course and before school breaks up. Some schools are going further and giving new contracts that begin in July, giving you valuable experience of the school and a salary over the summer holiday – a clear signal of good faith. These kinds of arrangements work well when designed to support an induction programme. They will give you a better idea of what to expect rather than spending the summer wondering what the new school will be like.

New teachers invariably looked back on time spent in their new school before the start of the new term as valuable. They wanted to find out what they could about the school, absorb the necessary information and identify their priorities for preparation and planning. Often they focused on the differences between their new school and the one in which they carried out training. One very obvious question is: are there gaps in subject knowledge arising from differences between schemes of work, textbooks and exam boards? For example, an English teacher made a list of unfamiliar set texts that she had not taught; an ICT teacher arranged to attend a short course on web authoring using software that she would need to know; a modern foreign languages teacher worked on her Spanish, a language she had not had opportunities to teach within her school placement. Other obvious points of comparison are the special features of the school or the new classes, for example, how schools differ in the ways in which they deal with pupil management, not just the written policies but how these seemed to be implemented. Other new teachers found out about special needs in classes they were going to teach. For example, a teacher going to work in a school that offered special support for hearing-impaired pupils made a point of visiting a support teacher and observing how teachers worked with hearing-impaired pupils in mainstream classes.

Your induction to the school might fall well short of the comprehensive provision described in this chapter. You might need to be persistent in getting the background information you need. Prepare a checklist of questions you need answering in advance of a visit and explain that these questions are important for you. You will be signalling that you take your job seriously. Be aware that if your visit is taking place at the end of the school year everyone will be tired and looking forward to the summer, so be sensitive and persistent. Look for opportunities to open up about your concerns and your need for support. This can be risky but may well pay off in the long run. For example, John felt relieved in talking about his concerns over class management:

> I had struggled with the class management in my placement and in the event I had only just scraped through. I did not feel confident about next year. It would have been easy to hide this from the new school but I wanted to be open. When I got round to talking to my induction tutor I told her there had been concerns in my training and what I really needed was a couple of days in the school observing and having procedures explained to me and that next term I would need early observation of my teaching and someone to pick up the difficulties from the start. I could tell she was a bit startled by what I had said, but she responded well. She must have said something to my head of department as there was a complete change of track. He stopped being so laid back and said he would monitor my lesson plans and come into lessons. As it turned out I got an observation from the induction tutor in the first week and she gave me some useful feedback on how I could make a more forceful impression at the start of the lesson, but overall she was quite positive. I felt by being up front and getting in early I had got the support I needed and started the year on the right foot. To be honest I think it made all the difference.

Spend the necessary time in advance of the new term sketching out overviews of work you want to cover and the first lessons you are going to teach. However, in retrospect, some teachers explained they felt they had over prepared and found themselves 'stale' and over committed to a set of lessons which, in the event, were not appropriate to the groups they were teaching.

For you to do

- If you are unable, or your school is unable, to arrange a teaching contract for you before the new term then take whatever opportunities you have to visit the school, to attend any end-of-year staff training and discuss your timetable. Where possible, observe the classes you are going to teach and devise a list of key administrative, support and subject teaching issues you need answering.

- Consider any differences between your training school(s) and this one – what do these differences mean for extending your subject knowledge, your planning, your assessment and your classroom teaching?

- Consider your end-of-year profile. What do you think will best help you address any goals or targets you have set?

- Be realistic. You will want to show you are eager but don't offer to do things unless you feel sure you can carry them out.

- Prioritise. You cannot prepare for everything, relax and enjoy your free time during the summer.

- Stay positive. Prepare for the difficulties ahead but try to recall why you wanted to go into teaching and what you are looking forward to doing.

Thriving not surviving

As a new teacher you are officially a newly qualified teacher starting your induction period. However, your pupils will not see you as newly qualified: they will be expecting to see what several of the teachers called a 'proper' teacher from day one. They will expect you to deal confidently with their questions, set out expectations of work and behaviour and deal with any difficulties with patience and good humour. The training period was a useful rehearsal for all this but both you and the pupils you taught knew this was a temporary arrangement and that ultimately someone else was going to take over. In your first year of teaching you now have sole responsibility for the class. This is, of course, what you wanted when you went into teaching. You can focus on building a long-term relationship with the particular set of young people that fate – or the vagaries of the catchment area – has brought you together with.

The challenge can seem daunting but as a new teacher you do start with advantages (Oberski *et al.* 1999). You have a fresh view of the difficulties facing the school. You might come in with a more positive outlook and might be willing to invest time in developing relationships with pupils. You might have reserves of energy you can draw on. You might have special skills such as experience of using ICT in your subject, a strength in a modern language arising from a year abroad which is still fresh in your mind, or up-to-date 'real world' experience you can refer to in your teaching. Your training might have given you opportunities to look at, and reflect on, recent developments in teaching. You might come to see this first year as exhilarating in a way you have rarely felt before.

Many books talk about surviving your first year of teaching (Nathan 1995; Thody *et al.* 2000), but as a new teacher you can look forward to thriving as much as surviving. Many new teachers talked about enjoying their first year of teaching, gaining particular satisfaction from the relationships they formed with the children they taught. Many took easily to their new role and took pride in the development of their teaching skills. Their experience of this first year of teaching confirmed that they had made the right choice of career, something that was bolstered by the positive reactions of the pupils they taught. They could see children in lessons who wanted to work, who listened to what they had to say and who responded to questions. They felt growing confidence in their teaching. They felt comfortable in the role of teacher. For example, Graham began to feel accepted by the pupils right away and noticed that even pupils who seemed disinterested in work were responding to his teaching:

> When you start and you know nobody, it can feel very lonely, so half the enjoyment is when pupils stop you in the corridor and want to speak to you, asking you questions about things they've done in lessons, or what they're doing next lesson. You get a sense you're beginning to make an impact. But you get the biggest satisfaction when you get through to someone who may have been a 'lost cause', someone who didn't have any interest in the subject. I really enjoy that. It's not just about they want to do the work but they want to know you as a person, they want to start taking part in what is going on again.

The picture is confirmed by Paolo reflecting on his first term in school:

> People tell me that the honeymoon period will pass. They (the pupils) will get fed up with me and me with them, but it hasn't happened. I have been wondering when it will stop but I have loved it.

Several, like Sam, made comparisons between teaching and jobs they had left behind:

> The contrast with my previous job is amazing – it sounds silly but I still feel I am on holiday from work, it is so absorbing, I never find myself watching the clock.

Even quite daunting difficulties were a source of satisfaction rather than disenchantment as long as they were overcome in the end. For example, Mary found the whole of the first half term a struggle but getting to the half-term break marked a turning point:

> I started in September and you're so conscious when you start that everyone knows you are the newest there and half of them are wondering if you're going to hack it. At the end of the first week I was counting the days until half term. When it arrived I was exhausted and think I spent the first two days sleeping. I know people were wondering if I was coming back, I didn't know myself, but just having that week off to take stock seemed to work. It all came together more easily after that and I am really glad I stuck it out.

For Gareth the process of settling in took longer:

> The major satisfaction this year has been knowing I can do it. This came home when I was taking over a class from a deputy head at Easter. It is not an easy school and he was a teacher they all looked up to. I had a big fight to get them to listen and to work. I felt they were looking back to him and judging me against someone else I could not match. But eventually they got used to me and the way I worked, they accepted me for the teacher I was. They are getting on well and I am enjoying it.

Shamina felt a particular sense of achievement in her relationship with pupils from Asian backgrounds in her school, a city school that was struggling to raise expectations and academic achievement:

> The Pakistani kids in the school are very close to you as a teacher. I don't know if it is the same elsewhere but here they want to know about you and they want to talk to you. They rely on you a lot and soon they are asking you, 'Miss, are you staying for the year?' They want you to stay. They see me as a role model, I think, because I am young and I'm Asian and I can tune into the culture, I have an idea of what is going on. The school uses me a bit. Other teachers ask me questions about festivals or marriages or whatever and I have translated things when parents have come into school. I wasn't sure about this at first but now I realise I can contribute a lot and when they ask me, they are taking an interest. They want to know more and it recognises what I can offer.

For many new teachers the feeling of being accepted was linked to particular moments in the year. Sharon started work in a school that followed what she saw as quite traditional teaching methods. She did not feel comfortable in the school until she felt confident enough to do things differently:

> On my PGCE placement I used this hot-seating idea. Basically, half the class would devise questions about the topic and then quiz the other half. I had not seen it done here and the department is a bit stuffy. I was a bit nervous about how the kids would react. But they went for it. That's when I realised that I could work here. I could try things out and it would work out.

Out-of-school activities such as field trips and adventure activities represented a high point for several teachers. Di, a modern languages teacher, found her first exchange trip abroad boosted her confidence:

> It had been very well organised and to be honest I felt a bit of a passenger at times. But it was good that they could see me in a different light, they could see how I got on with the other teachers and, maybe, they found we liked a bit of a laugh too. And I think they could see that what I was teaching them really did have some use and they could see I was doing all I could to

get them to make the best of their stay. I came away feeling that I could relate to these children after all and they could to me.

Satisfaction with your first year in school comes from knowing you have successfully taken on a new role, from the self-belief that you are making a difference, and from moulding the job to better fit your values and beliefs about teaching. Stresses and strains are inevitable but dealing successfully with challenges provides a sense of achievement not anxiety.

Focus question

- Consider your achievements as you go through your first term in your new school. What insight do these achievements give you about your aspirations as a teacher?

When it gets too much

Not all experiences of the first year of teaching are so positive and not every moment is one to be treasured (see, for example, some of the accounts of the first year of teaching in Hannam *et al.* 1976 or try the more recent observations of Gilbert 2004a). Like most new teachers you will probably experience some doubts about your career choice and you may have significant worries and concerns. These may be quite personal to you but some frequently recurring difficulties (Travers and Cooper 1996; Nathan 1995) include:

- feeling overwhelmed;
- the challenge of being accepted by pupils;
- relationships with colleagues;
- excessive working hours.

Feeling overwhelmed

You might experience the year as one in which you feel continually challenged by what is asked of you and generally feel alone and under-prepared. This is, after all, a new job, new work environment, perhaps a move to a new neighbourhood and, for some, their first 'proper' job. There is a mountain of administrative detail to take on at the same time as you are feeling wobbly about the role you are being asked to fulfil. Then there are the intangibles such as who can you rely on if you want help, who can you trust if you let your guard down and why do so many people assume you know things that you do not know? Several new teachers said that they felt completely overwhelmed. Sara explains:

> I don't think the placements can prepare you for the reality of starting your first year. I got a week's induction in the summer which was fine, but then suddenly there you are with a whole set of demands and there's something you need to carry out by yesterday. Going into school for the first day knocked me flat. I thought I knew what I had to do but I found there was so much more to learn. Yes, I felt nervous, scared. It was natural in any new situation, but it just went on and on like that.

Looking back on his first year Keith had not realised what it would entail:

> It was definitely a lot harder than I expected. There's a lot you do not see when you are on placement, you think you see it but you don't. It still comes as a shock when there are all these classes, they are your responsibility. On the PGCE there is someone to guide you along the way, but now it's all down to you and I was not really prepared for that aspect of it.

No matter how well organised you are, any routine for managing your work load can be shaken off course by further demands such as parents' evening or report writing, as Jenni found:

> You don't realise how long it takes until you do your first round of reports. I know it gets easier over time, you see other teachers and it's not that they don't care but they just get on with it. Me, I agonised over it at first. You want to say this one 'lacks attention in class' but then it comes back to you, doesn't it? If they lack attention that is my fault, well that is what I would say if I was the parent. If you say they are doing alright and they are not, you are covering something up. It goes on and on in your head. And then we are supposed to discuss these reports with parents and by the time you have been through one of those evenings you are no good for anything the next day.

In a similar fashion you may find your equilibrium disturbed by more unpredictable events, for example, in Alan's case the intrusion of a parent:

> It was early in the morning and I got in early to sort myself out for the day. It was winter and it was cold. I walked down the corridor to see this man ranting and waving a fist in front of our head of department. I was shocked as I had never seen anything like this in school and it gave me a perspective on the risks we take in teaching. I found out he was a parent arguing about how we had dealt with a problem with his son and he had lost it. He should not have been in the building. I can't explain but it shook me up. I had seen the school as my territory, but suddenly it did not seem safe. It took a while to feel OK again.

Several new teachers spoke about a crisis of confidence at some time during their teaching. Teaching is an emotional job and in order to do it well you need to feel emotionally secure in the community you are joining (a point made by many commentators on organisational behaviour, drawing on original work by Maslow 1970). Of course, some of the difficulties you experience might seem to have very little to do with school – ill health, a break-up with a partner, a wrong choice of flatmate – but if your confidence and self-esteem are knocked in school you might find consequences out of school, for example, withdrawing from friends and family. When it comes to school the key to your feelings about your first year of teaching almost certainly lies in your relationship with your pupils.

Classroom management

Classroom conflict probably has most power to puncture your confidence and self-belief. If you are having a difficult time in the classroom, colleagues can do only so much for so long to lift you. Of course, dealing with conflict is part of the job. The difficulty arises when you sense you are losing the conflict and feel a lack of control over the class. On a low level you might get a sense that pupils are not working as well as they could or should, that they are not listening when you speak, not engaging with classroom discussion and doing the minimum. In more difficult cases you might sense there is little direction and control in the class and some pupils are becoming rude and aggressive. This can easily lead to a vicious circle in which your

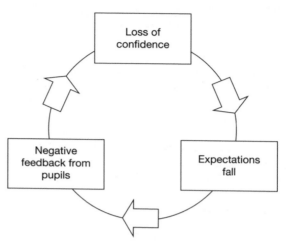

Figure 4.1 Teaching: a vicious circle

confidence is undermined; your enthusiasm and expectations drop; pupils become more negative about your teaching; which leads straight back to a greater loss of confidence (see Figure 4.1).

Here, three new teachers tell us about the difficulties they encountered. What would you do in their shoes?

The isolated class

Yasmeen had a successful school placement and started work in a challenging city school. Generally she felt successful in her work but one class in particular gave her difficulty:

> It has just been horrible teaching this class, it has demoralised me at times. The worst point was the kid who turned round and called me a bitch. That felt to me to be the lowest point of my life. There was another low-point, actually. Same class; Friday afternoon; thirty kids in the small room; it's ridiculous! It gets jam-packed in here, and it's not an ideal place to begin with. Everybody complains about it, they don't like the atmosphere, there's too many people in the room. They're a very behavioural problem class. They spend their time throwing paper round the room. I find it very hard to get anything out of them.

What happened?

In this case, Yasmeen was able to see this class as an isolated one. She kept focused on how well she was doing with the other classes and sought support from her head of department for the difficult class. She spoke to the head of year for this class who, in the event, made her feel inadequate because 'she was unable to control the class'. Over time the class became more accepting of her – she successfully 'toughed it out'. Her position in the school was boosted by the academic success of her other pupils and she stayed at the school and later became head of department.

Continual challenge

Tim struggled during his PGCE placements and found his first year as an NQT a challenge right from the start:

> My biggest achievement this year is being able to look back on it and say I've done the year. It took a long while to settle down, but there's been an awful lot of support from other NQTs and other staff and once the kids got more used to me, particularly the Y11, things got better. Project work has been the worst, there are Y11s with no project work to hand in, but A level teaching I've enjoyed – it was important to know that there were kids who could accept me and that has gone well.
>
> At the start I was blaming the students and I was right to do that, but at the same time I haven't made the rules clear enough or been consistent. I wasn't getting anywhere, the same arguments with the same kids. I felt out of control of the lessons, they were dictating what was happening. It's very difficult to regain ground once that has happened, you have to edge round them, renegotiate, and I don't want to be doing that again. One of them, if you sit by her, she will do it, but if you go away she stops, that is all you can say. I feel I spent too long negotiating with them at the start not telling them what I expected, and this has affected what they've learnt. So it's about my classroom management, but it's also about planning and balancing the lesson. You can't expect them to sit there for 20–30 minutes, they need variety, I need to really work on that.

What happened?

Tim successfully completed his first year and stayed at the school. Two things stand out. First, he needed and received a high level of support and the school seems to have done this without undermining his confidence. He felt he would not have completed the year without the support of year tutors and his head of department. They offered to talk to particular pupils and would go into difficult classes. He was not threatened by this and felt it sent an important signal to pupils at the school. Second, he learnt to go beyond blaming his pupils for their behaviour and looked to see what he could do to put things right. In his case this meant commitment to a set of rules in class and not giving up trying to enforce them. A further factor in getting through the year was the social side of school. He got on well with other new teachers in the school and played in the staff cricket team. This helped him relax from the challenges of the role.

Unable to cope

Sara's case was more difficult. She went to work in a very demanding city school. She had experienced some difficulties during her second PGCE placement, some of which she put down to her age, she was 21, and felt only a little older than the youngsters she taught. She found she could not handle the pupils in her new school:

> I made a wrong choice going to this school. It was an absolute sodding nightmare! They were really awful; every day I was in tears. I felt such animosity towards me particularly from the girls – I just wasn't prepared for it. I knew the school as I had been a student mentor in this school when I was at university so I knew the youngsters but now I was a teacher it was different. The girls saw me as a threat. They would say it is all right for you, but that was so unfair. I had struggled really hard to get where I had and they gave me no credit. If only they knew. I put so much into the job. I was really going for it. I worked all over summer and the hours! I was working 8 till 8, and sometimes 9, and I still wouldn't be able to get my act together to teach them. I was doing my break duty, lunch duty and running a lunch time club. In the end I wasn't really looking after myself. I couldn't go on. The school tried to be helpful, they offered support and gave me time off. They really wanted me to succeed but I had

enough. I had to go – I literally packed my bags and went back home to my mum's, without even thinking about it, and then started getting it together from there.

What happened?

Sara's case is a cautionary one. She was going to a school she knew – she had been a mentor on an undergraduate work experience scheme – and she had prepared her schemes of work thoroughly. She had high ambitions and a commitment to succeed. However, it had not worked out and she had got into a cycle of working harder and harder perhaps to compensate for the lack of success she felt in school. This was a futile strategy because it left her more stressed and vulnerable. In the end Sara left the school but very quickly found work in a less challenging environment where she successfully developed her career. Sara seemed to have received support and help from the school, but without direct practical mentoring and expert feedback on her teaching the challenge was overwhelming.

Coping with class management

If you find continued challenge to your teaching look back at previous advice and draw on your experience during your training programme. To reiterate an earlier point, there is a balance here between what you can do and what is out of your control. For example, Yasmeen did what she could with her class but saw many of the problems as beyond her. She may not have been entirely right about this, but it enabled her to cope in the short term and keep a sense of perspective. In contrast, a turning point in Tim's development as a teacher was the recognition that he had the responsibility for setting the ground rules for the class – something he had not been doing. The message here is to take the responsibility for your teaching but not the blame when things do not turn out as you hoped. Continue to be open about your difficulties. You might not want to be seen as a 'weak link' but, as in Tim's case, colleagues can help through work within tutor groups, observation of your teaching and simply through their presence at key times. Of course, appropriate support might not be forthcoming, as in Yasmeen's case, but you need to ask to find out.

Finally, try to stay positive and tough it out if you can. You might be surprised at how suddenly the class will come round to responding to you. If all else fails, at some point it is an option to decide that this is not the school for you. You might find, like Sara, that you go on to thrive in a different environment and good advice is to explore other schools or colleges before deciding teaching is not for you. Sometimes the realisation that you can leave might make it easier to renew your commitment to the school. If you do decide to leave teaching, try not to see your training as time wasted. You will have developed valuable skills for almost any career you might decide to take up and you will have an understanding of teachers and teaching that you could not have got in any other way.

Relationships inside school

You are not only faced with managing relationships with pupils; there are new relationships with fellow teachers to consider. Your key relationships are likely to be with your induction tutor and senior management team (SMT), your HoD, your departmental and other colleagues and, in particular, other new teachers in the school. Your relationship with your induction tutor may be a source of stress if you felt your induction arrangements were lacking. Perhaps you did not have the opportunity to get to know the school, the school did not offer you the emotional reassurance you needed, you were left wondering why they had appointed you. Perhaps the school was blasé about protecting your non-contact time, or showing that they did not feel they had a duty of care. Some teachers, like Karen, found induction tutors unsupportive and threatening:

> He was the last person you would want to go to if you wanted help, he would turn it all back on you. He made you feel if you were having problems it was your fault and I ended up just avoiding him.

Some teachers went further and talked about members of SMTs who pressurised them into taking roles. Jim, for example, was not ready to take on the role of managing a tutor group.

> Looking back I was wrong to say I could do it and it was wrong of them to ask me. I hadn't had the experience. The registration was OK but there were always forms to collect in or absence notes to chase up and your head was buzzing as you went into your first lesson, it was not the right preparation. Then I lost it in terms

of the PSHE lessons, it was a different style of working to what I was used to. The head of year explained it all to me but there seemed so little content to the lessons. You would have a question to discuss with the class but at times it was like getting blood out of a stone, other times you couldn't stop them talking but it was rarely about what they were supposed to be doing. Eventually I had to say I couldn't do it. There was all kind of pressure on me. I was told I was letting them down but I stuck to my guns. I decided I wanted out at the end of the year at that point.

Shamina felt that her SMT was unsympathetic as she tried to balance work and child care:

If there are no meetings I have to leave on time to pick my child up. The school wants us here for longer but I can't do it. I've given so many positive things to school, for them to question my commitment because of the way I manage this is ridiculous. One of them (a deputy head) still has a bee in her bonnet about it and this thing about school being a family. I'd say bullshit to that. They say we have to build an image of the school, but to me it's what you teach that's important and I know I am doing really well and managing my time properly.

It is likely that difficult relationships with your HoD, or members of your department, can be a greater source of anxiety than your relationship with your SMT, as the former is likely to impact on your day-to-day teaching. Some teachers felt undervalued by their HoD, their opinion was not sought and their timetables lacked examination classes, which seemed to be reserved for more experienced colleagues. In extreme cases teachers felt they had been given more difficult classes perhaps as a 'baptism of fire'. Megan, for example, found:

The key issue for me this year has been taking on his classes (a teacher who had left that year). I guess he had given up bothering. So for half my timetable at least there were these classes not used to working but all being told they were doing fine and on course for this or that. And I felt that everyone in the department thought I was moaning or being unhelpful about this or perhaps they were just embarrassed at what was going on but nobody helped me sort it out.

Sometimes the source of your disappointment in the department may be less tangible and although the school has been relatively helpful and supportive you have a sense of being in the wrong department or the wrong school. Jon felt he had not formed close relationships with other colleagues:

> I thought I would get to know the other teachers but it didn't work out. They knew I was a new teacher, but no one suggested going out to do this or do that. I am not paranoid about this, I expect they liked me enough but it put me under pressure as there wasn't the opportunity to chat about things.

There are many kinds of difficulty you may experience in your relationships with colleagues. At times you will find it easier not to confront these difficulties head on and you may find compensatory strategies, for example, by looking to a colleague for support rather than the induction tutor. However, you may have to take more serious issues to a union representative or LEA adviser. There is also an independent teacher support network offering a telephone helpline and online advice (this can be accessed at www.teacherline.org.uk). Look for opportunities to contribute to changing the culture of the school from below. For example, the atmosphere in some staff rooms, and relationships between staff, have been transformed with a significant intake of new teachers. You might find other new teachers a rich source of emotional and practical support.

Excessive workloads

You are almost bound to find your first year, and the first term in particular, exhausting. You are taking on a new role, new responsibilities, a fuller timetable than last year with more day-to-day responsibility. Planning for this is going to eat into your leisure time. Of course, some new teachers did the minimum in terms of preparation and marking while, at the other extreme, several had such high expectations that they created work routines which, as in Kevin's case, were unsustainable:

> I worked so many hours in the first term. I did all the usual things and more. I created resources for the school intranet. I put up notes on all my lessons and links where they could find out more – it was a bit of a hobby of mine so I didn't mind doing it. But it meant that I was working 60–70 hours in the week, and one day at least at weekends. In the end it was making me ill.

Sometimes departments were not as supportive or, as in Anne's case, were simply unaware of the pressure that she had piled on herself.

> I felt trapped by the enthusiasm I had shown at interview and these reports they had from my tutors. I knew I was good, everyone said I was good, but all the time when I started I thought the only way is down. I felt I had to be special, nobody told me to take it easy, and it took its toll. I felt washed out by the end of the first term, tearful, exhausted and not wanting to go back. I did go back of course but it was a really tiring year. I wouldn't want anyone to push themselves like that.

Jenny also found the hours she was putting in were excessive but believed that was the only way to do the job:

> For me this first year has been impossible and I am thinking of leaving. You cannot do it in the time they give. I am in here all hours and working at weekends. It is the project work which is a killer, you have to set targets in advance for each pupil, and then the marking. If you don't read it and follow it you can't set the targets. Don't get me wrong in terms of work it has been worth it, but you cannot do it all the time. The only thing which would keep me in teaching was more preparation time or much smaller classes.

Long hours in themselves were not always the problem. It was easy to make the commitment if you were swept along by the job, buoyed by the excitement of the challenge and a real sense of success. Some teachers, like Luke, willingly volunteered to take part in the out-of-school activities:

> This year we did the Duke of Edinburgh challenge and they organised some practice weekends. No one asked me, I wasn't geography or PE, but it is something I had done myself so you see I was keen to help. They were a bit surprised about that but I enjoyed it.

Problems arose when, as Bernard found, teaching a difficult class could leave you drained and it was difficult to pick yourself up to prepare for the next day:

I don't know what it is about that class, but it is not working out and it is not doing me any good. I do the whole day on Tuesday, I feel great and have something more when the bell goes at 3.30. But Wednesday I spend the whole day worrying about them, they are the last lesson, and I go straight home afterwards, dead on my feet.

Equally unsettling was when the effort seemed disproportionate or simply frustrating, as William found:

You don't realise until you start how much time you will spend filling in forms. You can get asked about an individual pupil and it can take 10 minutes to fill a report in. It all distracts me from the job I went into. There always seems to be another form in your pigeonhole. On top of this there is so much everyday marking and recording, much more than I expected. Does anybody see it? I doubt it. Then the meetings after school. They could put it on a piece of paper and hand it out, but people have to talk for the sake of talking.

There is no easy solution to the difficulties discussed by these teachers. However, you can try to fix the limit of your involvement with teaching. Before you start the new term think about the work routine that best suits you and how you are going to keep the demands of your new job in perspective. Paula, Daniel and Sukbir explain the routines they developed:

I can't face anything after the school day. I go to the gym and then eat and usually fall asleep for a while. Then I work until late so that I have got everything ready for the next day. I leave one day aside at the weekend and use Sunday afternoon to catch up with marking and anything else which must be done.

(Paula)

I stay behind at work until everything is done. I get in at 8.00 and finish at 5.00 and that is that. I try to make sure that I don't think about teaching when I am not in school but if I have had a bad day that is difficult.

(Daniel)

I have to leave school at 3.30 on the dot to pick up my child at the nursery. The marking and preparation I have to do at home once I have sorted her out and got her to sleep.

(Sukbir)

As far as possible stick to the hours you are prepared to work, and after that say no to yourself or to other people. This will be easier in some schools than others. The job is never ending. This will mean letting some pupils down, but you are letting them down far more if you are exhausted and you cannot get through the year.

Good management techniques include blocking off time for other aspects of your life. Set aside evenings when you aim to go out and give yourself at least a whole day switched off from school at the weekend. When school is closed for holidays, block in the first part of the break for school work, the rest of the time is for you. Talk to friends and family and find out if they feel you are withdrawing from them or neglecting them. These relationships are important, as Eddie discovered:

Then suddenly my wife said she was going to leave me unless she saw more of me. I think she must have said something to the head of department because I got the same message there, go home, work less. I don't think she was serious – at least I hope not – but she was right. I had to put limits on it.

Be strategic in your commitment to innovation and change. Identify lessons or areas of work in which your innovations are likely to have most success and be recognised by others. Some of the time, perhaps a great deal of the time, you are going to have to go along with things as they stand. Teaching is draining but as the new term gets under way try to identify those aspects of the job that are running you down most. It is not the hours you work but what happens in those hours that counts: if you are under great stress in the classroom your body needs time to recover – otherwise, in the long run your health will suffer.

Dealing with stress

The challenges you face and your reaction to those challenges are all aspects of stress. Stress is not bad in itself, overcoming challenge is a source of satisfaction not regret (Gold and Roth 1993; Moore 2004).

The negative association with stress arises when you feel unable to meet the challenge and when your reaction to the challenge is inappropriate. For example, it is understandable if you nearly always feel 'pumped up' as you go into class – so called flight or fight reactions – but this is not going to help you think through strategies for dealing with pupils and will affect your health sooner or later. Again, pressure of work might make you tempted to withdraw from social activity but this will cut you off from the very people who can help you get a clearer perspective on teaching. If you find your first year of teaching particularly stressful try to identify what you need to address right away and discuss possible solutions; block off free time; be realistic about what you can achieve at work. Contact the Teacher Support Network (www.teacherline.org.uk) for further guidance. Teachers generally have a strong 'internal locus of control' (Rotter 1989) and a belief in their ability to overcome constraints and make a positive impact on young people. The trick is to hold onto this belief without engaging in self-recrimination or despair when the extent of the challenge becomes clearer.

Summary

This chapter has looked at:

- what you can do to prepare for the first year;
- positive experiences of teaching;
- the challenges you will face;
- dealing with stress.

Chapter 5

Developing your teaching in your first year

The previous chapter described how many new teachers enjoyed their first year of teaching and welcomed taking full responsibility for the classes they taught. Most felt they became established in school and, to a greater or lesser extent, had been accepted by the classes they taught. This chapter looks at how teachers developed their teaching in the first year and will help you:

- identify how your teaching has progressed;
- identify opportunities for training and support;
- consider the CEPD process;
- consider what is meant by meeting the induction standards.

You and your progression as a teacher

Over the year new teachers spoke about how their confidence and knowledge of pupils developed. Here, Sandra describes how she learnt more about the way that particular classes approached her subject:

> As you do it for longer the more confident you are in what you are doing. Some of it is being more decisive – so I don't suppose I am starting a lesson exactly as my tutor said but I don't care. It fits into place and the pupils go along with it. Some of it is just changing to fit who you are teaching.

While Janet, a science teacher, found she could predict the difficulties pupils would have with a topic more easily:

> I knew from last year that they would find this business of interpreting graphs difficult. I worked out you needed to put it in a

context they can relate to more easily. For example, I got them plotting what happens to the temperature of a cup of coffee over time and then more difficult things like marathon runners, plotting the distance they travelled against time or their speed against time. The examples in the book are too difficult and they can't find a way into understanding the concepts.

Most new teachers felt they developed their subject knowledge. They knew the material better and could see it more clearly from a child's point of view.

They had a feel for when would be a good time for introducing a topic, and, like Manjit, a design and technology teacher, a better idea as to how much time they had to explain topics to children before they switched off:

When I introduced the project brief for the first time I spent far too long talking. I tried to go through it all at once which was right in theory but in practice they gave up following me. This was my approach last year but here it did not work out as I had expected. So now I am trying much more to do brief intro-ductions and calling back the class during the lesson as and when I need to.

Several teachers explained how they understood the assessment arrangements more clearly and felt they were able to make better judge-ments on pupils' work. For Daniel taking the pupils for the whole year had been important:

Some of it is taking a wider view of pupil progress. On placement you are asking yourself how much has this person achieved in this lesson or this week or even six weeks or more. Now you have the whole year to look back on and you can see the whole picture much more clearly, you get a better feel for the effort they are putting in and what you should be expecting them to do.

Most felt they had developed their classroom teaching. For example, Julie was able to pinpoint how she had succeeded in providing an entry point for all pupils:

Over time you realise that some pupils are not getting it and you become more and more aware of the language difficulties which the weaker ones face. You have to find ways of making it clear what you want them to do, being aware of who can support who and checking to see that everyone has made a start.

Most teachers had a very practical 'go with what works' approach to teaching their new classes that built on their previous knowledge and experience, as summarised in Box 5.1.

Box 5.1 Examples of progression in teaching

Focus	At beginning of the year recognised the importance of . . .	Over the course of the year recognised the importance of . . .
Decisiveness (Sandra)	Setting out clear guidelines	Signalling confidence and control
Explanation (Jane)	Clarity in explanation and drawing attention to key words	Making context more accessible
Balance between whole-class and individual activity (Manjit)	Demonstration to the whole class and whole-class discussion	Adjusting to pupils' attention span
Reporting (Daniel)	Giving formative feedback	Wider evidence on which to base judgements
Entry point for all pupils (Julie)	Making work accessible to all pupils	Not just planning entry points but monitoring pupils and responding quickly

It is easy to put developments like these down to 'learning by experience' but experience is not enough in itself. New teachers spoke of the work that went into reflecting on what had gone on in class – something that Schön in writing about reflective practice calls reflection on action (Schön 1987) – and the planning that goes into developing new ways of teaching. The importance of gauging pupil feedback was discussed in Chapter 3 and this is equally important in your first year. As a newly qualified teacher you will probably carry out evaluations of your lessons in a much less formal manner. You will not have the time for writing up detailed notes and it might be less likely that anyone is going to look at them. However, try to ask yourself focus questions familiar from your training about your teaching (e.g. what went well, what went less well, what would you do differently?) and about pupils and their learning (e.g. how would this lesson appeal to different types of learner, what is difficult in learning this topic?). This might lead you into developing new strategies for pupil self-evaluation. For example, Jon found pupil diaries helped him check on pupils' misconceptions:

> One aspect of my teaching that has really come in this year is pupil self-assessment. I am much more into giving them time to think about what they are doing and this lets me know what is difficult for them or maybe what I have not explained very well. I have been using pupil diaries, simple ideas like traffic lights at red if you don't understand, yellow if maybe, and green, no problem. At first it was a bit cumbersome but they have got into it now and I am picking up a lot more on the progress they are making.

Some new teachers try to get direct feedback on their teaching from pupils themselves, though, like Helen, a business studies teacher, they had to feel pretty confident to do this in the first place:

> I had this sixth form class I was not getting on well with, nothing major, I just felt they were not working very hard for their exams and were putting more in with other teachers they had. So we had this long talk together and I told them about my concerns and asked if there was anything they wanted me to do different. I was surprised how well they took to it and it really worked. Some approached it on the level of 'Don't worry, miss, we know we have been messing about too much.' But when they thought about it they said it would really help them if I could be crystal clear when the project had to be in by and could be clearer about how each part of the project was to be assessed. It sounded obvious when they said it but it kind of broke the ice with the group and they really did some good work.

You can establish classroom routines such as scanning the class at regular intervals, circulating the class and making sure you speak to each pupil at some time. Try to 'think on your feet' and make quick adjustments to your lesson plan based on what you have picked up by monitoring pupils (this is described as reflection in action by Schön). Here, Jenni describes the quick adjustments she makes in her teaching:

> You get started with the lesson and you can see they are not into talking so you don't do it, you just tell them to get on with it and try again later. Or you pick up they are bored so you vary the activity, give them a different angle on it, or they didn't get it so you find another way to tell them. You've got to be prepared to try it out and if it goes wrong at least you've had a go.

You have many opportunities to try new approaches but many new teachers feel there is less time for experimenting and innovating than they had supposed. One reason is that they are teaching a fuller timetable. Some new teachers are inhibited by their status in school – they were expected to try things out during their training but it was too risky now they were supposed to be 'proper' teachers. As seen in the previous chapter, much will depend on how you fit into the department. It might be much harder to innovate if you are moving away from styles of teaching that your pupils are used to or if you are in a department with a controlling HoD.

For you to do

Discuss, with a colleague and/or your induction tutor, the ways in which you evaluate your teaching and identify ways of extending your evaluations. Set yourself goals or targets to develop your teaching based on these evaluations.

Support for new teachers

Teaching is rare among professions in what is asked from you so early in your career. Nonetheless, as an NQT in England you are entitled to a reduced timetable (90 per cent of a qualified teacher's) and to use your non-contact time specifically for activities related to induction and career development. You are entitled to a tutor, or 'induction tutor', who will help you get the most out of your year. This tutor has responsibility for helping you to organise an individualised programme with regular observation of your teaching and opportunities to observe other teachers and attend in-service events. You will also have a named contact at the LEA (or ISCTIP if you are working in the independent sector) with whom you can raise any concerns. Your entitlement is spelt out by the Teacher Training Agency (TTA 2003d) and you can go both to the TTA and DfES web sites for further details. The *Times Educational Supplement* (TES) web site has several sections for new teachers including 'Ask the Expert' and a 'New Teachers' Forum', and the TES also regularly publishes guides for new teachers. You might also be interested in looking at induction tutor guides to your first year such as Bubb (2000) and Bleach (2000), both of whom give detailed advice on target setting, and Cowley (2003), Nathan (1995), Thody *et al.* (2000) as accessible survival guides.

In spite of the optimism expressed by the Teacher Training Agency in discussing induction arrangements, new teachers' experiences remain very varied.

As a new teacher you will almost inevitably learn a great deal by trial and error but your development is made much easier if you have opportunities for observation, for reflection, target or goal setting, monitoring and coaching. Jamila describes how she was supported in developing her work on questioning:

> In my school we meet as a group of new teachers with our induction tutor every week and we discuss what's bugging us and what we are not happy with. We spent a long time on pupil behaviour last term but this term I have looked at question and answer. This came up when the induction tutor saw me teach. She suggested I tried to find ways of getting all the class thinking about questions I was asking and address different types of question to different pupils. She got me to observe her lesson and write down the questions she asked and we talked about what I thought worked and what I wanted to do. She got me to rehearse the questions I was going to ask before the next lesson she was going to observe. She came in and gave me really detailed feedback and she checked later to see that I was following through on all this.

This school had created an environment in which new teachers could easily talk about their concerns and in which senior teachers were eager to demonstrate classroom styles and techniques and help coach new teachers. In contrast, some teachers received very little in the way of support – like Peter they were left to get on with it:

> We had a tour of the school on the day before the pupils came back but that was it. The deputy head said come and find me if there are any problems. I think someone came in to observe me but they went away again and I didn't really get the chance to see other teachers or go on courses. It was disappointing really.

This was echoed by Dave, a PE teacher, who felt the whole year had been a struggle without anyone to turn to:

> I look back and there was nothing there to help me. At times I didn't know which way to turn. I was not getting through to them (the pupils), I didn't want it to be like this. I wanted someone to stick their neck out and say this is why I think you are going wrong, have you tried doing this, let me show you how to do that. Because I just didn't know what to do, whether I should come in harder or be more matey, whether to do more or fewer team games, whether to give in and have them do football all the time.

Between these two extremes a common experience was that schools were slow in coming forward with support and guidance but reacted well when things were going wrong. The previous chapter described how colleagues rallied round Tim when he had difficulties managing his class. Carlton describes a similar story in which a senior teacher, George, acted with both assertiveness and sensitivity:

> A key moment for me was teaching a very disaffected group and I just had it, I walked out. I didn't know where I was going and I bumped into George, the deputy head. He sat me down, talked me through it and went to the class. He was great. He gave them a right talking to, he was really angry or at least pretended to be angry, said it was quite unacceptable, they were here to learn and I was the one who could teach them. For the next few lessons after that George was great. He would make a point of being around when I was teaching, he didn't need to go in, they just knew he was about, he was supporting me but not making a big thing of it. Looking back, it all could have backfired, but it worked, it showed the school backed me and wanted me to succeed.

This was an example of well judged support and you might be surprised how far people will put themselves out for you in your first year. Try not to feel it is all on your shoulders. Nonetheless, it was disappointing that in Carlton's case his problems had not been picked up earlier by his induction tutor or that Carlton had not felt able to talk about his difficulties with the class. Carlton could have been helped to address the conflict in the class by getting early feedback on his teaching.

It is not always easy to balance your demands with those of the wider school. Schools are busy places. Your school might start out with the best of intentions about your training programme, but teachers go off sick, new initiatives arrive, inspections are announced, exams are being taken, there is always something else to do. And if you are getting along alright there is very little incentive for you or management to monitor you or your training programme very closely. If you feel you have 'cracked it' as a teacher then you are very likely to be learning so much so quickly you are probably not so worried about talking about what you are doing, or having anyone in to see how you are doing it. You might not see the point of taking time away from your class observing another teacher or attending an in-service event even if these are really important strategies for your development. Without you pushing, induction tutors and senior managers might leave you to get on with it. Getting by is alright but this will not put you on track to reaching your full potential as a teacher.

However, you might find that your school is genuinely working hard at providing you with support and training, but simply does not know the best way to help. For example, like many new teachers Julie had been given the chance to observe another lesson:

> I was worried about my classroom management and they arranged for an observation of the deputy head's lesson. But it was hopeless. What good was that for me? All these pupils I had been having difficulty with, were good as gold in his lesson. It was a great lesson and he is a great teacher but I learnt nothing. I just felt hopeless. I couldn't get the work out of them and there he was doing it effortlessly.

In a similar vein Sharon had found those observing her lesson had not taken the time to get to know her or what she was trying to achieve:

I got this note saying they were going to see my lesson. I knew what they wanted to see, a three-part lesson – an introduction, a middle and an end. But I felt why should I alter what I was going to do to please them? I ended up getting bad feedback on my teaching, but I couldn't care less. Looking back I was being childish about it but they had not tried to involve me in what they were doing.

What can you draw from this range of experience? One clear message is if you are being well supported in your school show your appreciation and extract every advantage from the arrangements made for you. If you are unhappy with the support and training provided for you, bring this up with your induction tutor. This might be quite uncomfortable for both of you. Try to focus on what would help you to develop in the future rather than putting them on the defensive about what has been failing in the past. Be positive and proactive; for example some new teachers organise peer observations with other new teachers in the school and others find enormous value in seeing colleagues who trained with them last year in another school. (A music teacher, David Elliot, describes the importance of peer support in an article published some time ago but still relevant (Elliot 1984).) Then there is the day-to-day working with colleagues. You can continue to learn through talking to colleagues, 'picking up tips' often in informal settings. Sometimes the teaching of a class is shared, and this gives added opportunities to discuss ideas with more established colleagues. As in your training year there are opportunities for in-service sessions both in and out of school. Work out your own programme of observation of lessons and identify the courses you want to go on. It will be in everyone's interests to create a programme that you think will be effective. If difficulties remain you might want to discuss these with your union or professional association representative or with your local education authority adviser.

As with school support there are mixed reports on the training provided by LEA for new teachers. The structure and details of programmes differ from one LEA to another and schools differ in the importance they attach to it. For example, attendance was compulsory for some teachers and in school time, others were offered twilight sessions and it was up to them if they attended. A typical programme might consist of sessions based on:

- a welcome to teaching in the LEA: for example, an introduction to advisory and support staff, description of the range of schools and educational provision in the authority, courses offered, who to turn to if you need help;

- developing your teaching: for example, a review of key themes during your training programme and how you can draw on your career entry and development profile to design your training programme, and sharing of key concerns with other new teachers;
- managing pupil behaviour: for example, issues in classroom management, discussion of latest LEA and government advice;
- teaching your subject: for example, a meeting confined to new teachers of your subject in which you compare and contrast approaches in your school and discuss any latest developments;
- catering for special needs: for example, exploration of the range of special needs and the support available to meet them;
- cross-curricular themes: for example, ICT, numeracy and literacy.

Most teachers seemed to value the opportunity to meet teachers from other schools at these sessions and found ideas and guidance that seemed easy to apply to their particular classes. In contrast, some sessions were criticised for being too general and not easy to relate to teaching a particular subject. Not surprisingly, the response to individual tutors or course leaders varied as well. Overall, a message here is to use LEA provision to share ideas with other teachers and get to know what the LEA can do for you. If you can be proactive in saying what you would like a particular course to cover this may help both you and the person or people leading the course.

The CEPD process

The CEPD document referred to in Chapter 3 can be a useful reference point in meetings with induction tutors. Towards the end of your training programme (transition point 1) you were expected to comment on your achievements and areas to develop. At your first meeting towards the very start of your first year in school (transition point 2), you are expected, among topics of your own choosing, to discuss your most important professional development priorities during your induction period and changes in your priorities since completing your training. An exercise like this is going to help you if it raises aspirations and points to targets to develop your teaching, and if you are going to get help in achieving those targets. Reflection, action and support are more important than filling in the forms. At the end of the first year the CEPD process envisages that you will have an opportunity (transition point 3) to look back on the action points developed both in formal and informal meetings. Again, a series of focus questions is provided. When managed well this final meeting can help you become more aware of your progression as a teacher and help you focus on support and challenge in the coming year. Here, Sue talks about the encouragement her induction tutor gave her to take on teaching advanced level courses:

> My last meeting with my induction tutor was very useful and got me thinking about teaching on the vocational advanced courses. I thought it would be too soon, there is so much riding on it for the pupils and it was all new to me. But talking to him I realised that it was not all on my shoulders and the teaching could be shared. I had left it too late to observe classes, but I signed up for a session that the exam board were running. I talked it all through with my head of department and was given joint responsibility for one group next term. I am looking forward to it and it will give me more strings to my bow as a teacher. I don't think this would have happened unless they had encouraged me.

CEPD transition points – a scenario

Chapter 3 described a student teacher, Claire, who identified her strengths at transition point 1 as working with pupils with EAL, teaching at post-16 and innovative approaches in the classroom. Areas in which she wanted more experience included classroom management, tutor group work, diagnosing pupil misconceptions and post-16 teaching. Claire's first formal CEPD meeting with her induction tutor started with a discussion as to how she was settling into, and contributing to, the department and whether her teaching timetable was appropriate. Together, they went on to discuss the focus questions (these are abridged from the original document and italicised) within the CEPD process. Claire summarised the main points below:

At the moment, what do you consider to be your most important professional development priorities during your induction period?
Looking back at my transition point 1, I would still like to develop more positive approaches to managing children and would like to observe and get feedback from teachers. I feel that my introduction to the role of the tutor has already started and going well. I feel that I have made a good start to teaching at the post-16 level, but some

of the topics are new. Feedback on my teaching so far has been OK but I have concerns over the pace and challenge in the lesson.

How have your priorities changed since transition point 1? For example, are there any new needs and areas for development?
In general no new areas. The process has been made much easier by working here over July and I started the new term feeling I knew my way around school, the department and the schemes of work. This is a less academically successful school in terms of raw exam results than my placement school and I have had to adjust some of my teaching without lowering my expectations. The range of ability is an issue here as there are much broader bands or sets so I would like to look at differentiation by task, not just by outcome. I could look at this in more detail in spring term.

How would you prioritise your needs across your induction period?
My priority is to develop positive strategies for classroom management. I have made a good start and if I can maintain this I will have a base to develop further. I know classroom confrontations undermine me. If I can get early feedback on my teaching this will help my confidence. My next priority is feedback on my post-16 teaching. I saw it as a strength but I want that confirmed and I want to make sure I have understood the syllabus as it is new.

What preparation, support or development opportunities do you feel would help you move forward with these priorities?
I respond well to feedback on my teaching, I welcome observation. I would like to go on courses to improve my subject knowledge.

Based on the discussion, Claire and her tutor were able to work out a training programme for the first term (see Box 5.2). The plan was designed to fit onto one side of paper so that record keeping would be straightforward and easily accessible. The plan did not cover the informal training carried out as a matter of course within the department. In a fourth column Claire later noted a key point to come out of the training event.

There are several strengths to this training programme: the variety of events (in-service, observing and being observed); targets that were identified, discussed and monitored; and the combined involvement of induction tutor, HoD and a further colleague. The written plan is rudimentary but usefully maps out activities and actions.

Box 5.2 Claire's training programme

Goal	Training event	Actions
Week 1 Understand how LEA can support me	Meeting LEA	Sign up for subject in-service at teachers' centre
Week 2 Identify strengths and areas to develop in my class management	Observation by induction tutor	Clarity in transition between activities. Explicit directions for pupils
Week 4 Evaluate progress on addressing class management targets	Observation by HoD	Previous points addressed. Don't lose focus on rules for entry, seating, leaving classroom etc.
Week 6 Evaluate post-16 teaching	Observation by departmental colleague	Focus on productive relationships with pupils, key is making sure pupils get the assessment criteria
Week 8 Evaluate post-16 teaching	Observation of departmental colleague	Develop student-friendly guide to assessment, use peer assessment
Week 10 Evaluate post-16 teaching	Observation by HoD	Continue using new assessment strategies, attend in-service offered by exam board, register for exam board's online discussion forum
Week 13 Review	Meeting with induction tutor	Acknowledge progress. Plan for next term

Towards the end of her first year (transition point 3) Claire was able to reflect on her strengths and further areas to develop in a formal meeting with her induction tutor. Again, the italicised questions are taken from the original CEPD document (TTA 2003c) – though check the web site for changes in the procedure year on year.

Thinking back over your induction period, what do you feel have been your most significant achievements as a newly qualified teacher? What have been your key learning moments? What prompted your learning on these occasions? Which aspects of your induction support programme have you particularly valued and why?

My most significant achievement has been being able to do it – to manage all my classes, get on top of the administration, assess pupils work reliably and contribute to the department as a whole. I have settled in the classes I teach and get on well with my colleagues. I am particularly pleased by my work at post-16 as this was new for me and I taught it confidently and got good feedback. I have been helped considerably by paired teaching of this class so although we don't teach together there is someone else who knows the pupils, who I can show my work to and share ideas with. I have learnt best by planning in detail and getting help when I needed it. I have gained most by peer support, particularly the support of another teacher in the department (not my HoD). Observations have been useful and *some* of the sessions at the teachers' centre have been good – easy to apply in my teaching.

How have you built on the strengths you identified at the end of your initial teacher training? What evidence is there of your progress in these areas?

At the end of my training programme I thought my strengths were working with pupils with EAL. I have had a coordinating role for EAL in my department. I described myself as an innovative teacher but I don't think I have been this year, I haven't had the time for planning.

When you look back over your induction action plans and your records of review meetings, which objectives do you feel have been achieved and why? Are there any areas where you are less satisfied with your progress? Why do you feel this is? What further actions will you take in these areas? What further preparation or support do you feel you will need?

Overall I have been very pleased with my progress and feel I have addressed all the priorities for development. I realise that I have not been so successful with all classes and would like to investigate teaching

Y8s and Y9s more carefully. I am not getting them on task early enough and am disappointed in some of the work they have done. I would like to investigate whether other teachers feel the same way about these year groups and if there is something I could do better. I would benefit most from seeing other teachers and teachers in other departments.

Have any of the objectives, aspirations and goals that you outlined at transition points 1 and 2 not been addressed during your induction period?
My chief objective was to settle in the school and I have successfully done that.

Thinking ahead to the class(es) you will teach and the responsibilities you will be taking on next year, what do you feel are the priorities for your professional development over the next two or three years?
Next year my timetable is fine. I will be a form tutor next year and feel I have been led into this well and I am ready to do this. I will be taking exam classes into their second year of GCSE and A level, I feel prepared for this and I am looking forward to it. A priority is to find time to think again about some of the things we did during my training, such as the work on plenaries, I don't want to become stale in my teaching.

What options are you currently considering for professional and career progression? What could you do to help you move towards achieving these?
I feel that my career is on track and in the long term I would like to become an AST. I have had a lot to get on with this year and next year I have enough of a challenge in becoming form tutor and teaching a full timetable.

Focus questions

- How far have you addressed the areas for development signalled at the three CEPD transition points, or other career entry document, in use in your school?
- What opportunities are there for career progression in the school?
- What support and training would best help you in your second year?

Meeting the induction standards

Arrangements for assessing teachers in their induction year have changed over time and at one stage the induction year was even dropped. The present arrangements are explained on both the DfES and TTA web sites (the addresses of which are in Appendix C). Briefly, you are expected to complete your induction over three terms, though this may be calculated on a 'pro rata' basis if you work part time. The induction period may be extended in exceptional cases, but once begun induction must be completed within five years. If you are working in an independent, an overseas or a non-mainstream school you might want to get further advice on completing your induction (for details, again, go to the TTA web site). The induction standards relate closely to the Qualifying to Teach (QtT) standards with which you are already familiar from your training programme. There are six standards in the new induction arrangements in England but these are seen in the context of a general requirement to go on meeting, and further developing, the QtT standards. The six standards focus on:

- professional values and practice;
- knowledge and understanding;
- teaching: special educational needs; teaching: liaising with parents and carers;
- teaching: working as part of a team;
- teaching: securing appropriate behaviour.

The pros and cons of a standards approach have been discussed earlier; look for opportunities to discuss your understanding of these standards with your induction tutor. Where possible, collect examples of your best work, lesson plans, written feedback to pupils, teaching materials, photographs and video recordings if you have them. Again, worst case scenarios involve an induction tutor and new teacher 'ticking off' a checklist of statements that seem to have little relevance to their teaching.

If you are feeling comfortable in your new school and the feedback you have been getting has generally been positive, then you are unlikely to be too concerned about the summative assessment of your teaching. The whole point of the induction arrangements becomes focused on formative assessment – how you can go on improving your teaching.

As Daniel explains:

> I knew things were going well, I got on with the classes and was not aware of any major problems. The training programme was mixed. I went to some events and talked a lot with my subject leader and other people in the department. I remember them showing me a piece of paper which I had to sign each term which I think said I was meeting the standards but that didn't concern me. But I remember we did talk about things like differentiation and I did try out some useful ideas.

A summative assessment of your teaching takes place at a meeting between you and your induction tutor and or the headteacher towards the end of each term. At the end of the year your headteacher will make a judgement about your progress and a recommendation to the LEA as to whether you are on course to meet the induction standards. The vast majority of new teachers have a successful induction period and the formal process requires little more than a 'signing off' by the headteacher, and yourself. Later, the head's decision is ratified by the LEA which informs your headteacher, the General Teaching Council for England (see Appendix C) and the DfES.

If, however, you are worried about your progress and have been forewarned that you are at risk of failing to meet the induction standards then you need to seek advice from your induction tutor during your induction year. Don't wait until it is too late. Find out which aspects of your teaching are causing concern: What is the school putting in place to support you and what further feedback are you getting on your teaching? Your school has a duty to forewarn that you are 'at risk' and to offer you appropriate support. If you feel you are being judged unfairly then seek advice from your union representatives and from your local authority adviser. Make sure you have accurate details of the support you have been given, particularly if you think you have grounds for complaint.

A point made over again by teachers was that the key to a successful induction programme lay in how it was carried out; for example, the quality of the discussion, the engagement of mentors and outcomes from observation and coaching, rather than the formal recording of events.

Focus questions

•   Do you have any concerns about meeting the induction stand-
    ards? Discuss these with your induction tutor.

Summary

This chapter has looked at:

•   progression in your teaching;
•   support for new teachers;
•   the CEPD process;
•   the induction standards.

A key message has been to be proactive in identifying suitable
training opportunities.

Chapter 6

Developing your teaching in your second year

The previous chapters have been largely focused on your immediate concerns as a student teacher and as a new teacher settling into school. They stressed the importance of finding the right school and of taking advantage of opportunities for professional development. Your experience of your first year is going to influence how you approach your second year. You might, for example, go into your second year feeling very confident of meeting new challenges, or you might have found the first year a struggle and feel very uncertain that you want to continue. You might feel ready to embrace further responsibility in your department or you might be quite content to focus on your own classroom teaching. Whatever your particular circumstances, you now have greater experience and a sense of 'having been there before'. We look at the implications of this for your confidence, your developing teacher skills, your status and your future role in teaching.

This chapter will help you:

- prepare for the start of your second year;
- identify developments in your teaching;
- address continuing areas of concern;
- prepare for taking on new responsibilities;
- consider the pros and cons of moving school.

Starting the new term

You start the new year with a great deal more experience and more knowledge about your school; even if you have moved school, you will still have a great deal of experience on which to draw. Whatever the trials and tribulations of your entry into teaching, you will probably find that you will begin the new term with greater confidence. This will come from your own efforts to establish yourself in school but you will also be influenced by differences in the way other people react to you. It seems an obvious point, but it does come as a surprise, that at the start of your second year there are likely to be teachers with less experience than you. You might be surprised at how the new intake of newly qualified teachers finds you. Shamina explains:

> It was weird on the training day before school we started back in September. I remember how it had been for me the year before and now there was a bunch of new teachers sitting together. I remember how we were and this year feeling, 'Oh I'm not there, I'm not with them.' You almost feel up there because you've made it. Talking to them I said I had qualified last year and they said, 'No way.' They could not believe it and that makes you feel good that they see you as someone with that confidence and experience.

If staying put, you will have become more established in the eyes of older colleagues who realise that you are putting down roots in the school. Bob focused on the reactions of colleagues to his change in status:

> I am much more confident this year. You know that you are not an NQT (newly qualified teacher) and people change their attitudes towards you. I have a tutor group this year and when other teachers see you have got that and a full timetable it makes you feel you are a full part of the school.

Your position in the school might have become more visible by taking on new responsibilities. Marie describes the effect of introducing a new A level into the school:

> I set up a new advanced level in psychology last year. It was something I wanted to see introduced into school and they were very helpful in getting it running. I think this changed how people saw me, certainly the students seemed to think I had some responsibility now, they are very aware of things like this. I had to do a presentation at a sixth form evening for parents and students last term, just to say why we were doing the course and to speak to me if they wanted to know more. The head came up and was very complimentary and said he was pleased with the way

I had presented it. This really helped me feel I was making a contribution.

Another way you might become more visible to colleagues is if you have been teaching exam classes. In most schools exam results have a high profile, something that new teachers were aware of, and sometimes disturbed by, as Mathew explains:

> My results were alright and I could see other people had taken this in and I did grow in confidence. But I still feel very mixed, so much is left to chance. You could have a bad year one year, a good year the next, there is so much that comes into it. We could be a lot more supportive of each other.

The biggest change for many teachers in their second year is the sense that pupils accept them far more readily than before. In some schools turnover is so high that pupils felt particularly warm to teachers who stayed on – Shamina again:

> In our school they are on at you all the time, 'What are you doing miss, are you staying here?' and when I finished the first year they gave me a card and a present and they seemed so pleased to see me back. It doesn't stop them from having a go at me or me at them, but it is so much easier now than before.

Joe gave an example of feeling more at ease with his tutor group at the start of the second year:

> I can certainly say that I feel a lot closer to my tutor group this year. I think the residential we did with them in the summer term really made a difference and I think that's how I got through to them and how it became much easier to teach them. It takes time and you need to make the effort, it does work. There are certain teachers who have been here a long time and they will never really get through to them, because they have never really made the effort.

Preparation

Your preparation for the new term began towards the end of your induction year. Here was your opportunity to observe classes, to address gaps in your subject knowledge, to find out about special needs in classes you are likely to teach, observe new schemes of work being taught. You will also have benefited from countless unplanned conversations with colleagues about their classes and their teaching. No matter how well prepared you were first time round there will be a lot less catching up to do this year.

You will almost certainly want to use what you have learnt about your pupils in planning your first meetings with your new classes. One example was provided by Hope, a teacher in her second year who felt that she could plan better, so that all pupils could feel successful:

> They tell you all the time that how you start off with a class is really important but it all happens so quickly the first time around and then it's gone. This year I have really paid attention to getting it right. You can plan those first lessons properly because you know what to expect. This year I made sure I covered the topics I was really confident about, so I could spend my time thinking about how they were responding, who I needed to watch, who was going to have difficulty. I made sure that I pitched it so that everyone could get something out of these first lessons, I didn't want anyone switching off. I really followed through on the homework too so that they got into a groove. I know it is all going to slip over the year but the point is you want them to get into the habit of being positive, 'Yes I can do this' and 'I will learn something in this lesson' and this will make the rest of the year easier.

Meanwhile, Jonathan, following advice in Wragg (1995), tried to focus on re-establishing guidelines and expectations with his classes:

> The big difference between this year and last year is that my Y9 class have moved on. They had, they really got to me. I didn't enjoy the lessons and neither did they. From February onwards I was looking forward to losing that class. I stuck at it the best I could but I had enough to be honest. I felt I've been waiting to get a second chance. So this year I have really hammered away at these new classes, how they come into the class, how they need to get down to the work, there has been no let up. It has gone a lot better than I thought it would and I don't have any classes which have got on top of me like last year.

Focus questions

- At the start of your second year look back at your CEPD or other review you undertook towards the end of last term. Remind yourself of your strengths and your training and development goals, discuss these with a colleague or mentor.
- Review your planning for your first week of teaching. Are you giving opportunities for all pupils to feel successful in these first lessons? How are you communicating rules and expectations of classroom behaviour?

A coming together of confidence, recognition and expertise?

If the second year is going well, you might feel a 'coming together' of confidence, knowledge and skills and recognition from others. This left Bethan feeling in control:

> Yes, definitely, I feel in charge. Last year I wasn't, but now I think I'm so confident that I can control any situation. If suddenly a fire alarm goes off or someone comes in late or the equipment fails, I know what to do. I don't think, 'Oh my God what do I do?' I just naturally get on with it. If there are people moving around I just say right you lot are doing this, you are sitting here and you are doing that, I tell them bluntly but I know how to handle it, how to say what to whom.

Mark made the point that he no longer felt he was trying to fit in all the time – he had the confidence to assert his own authority in the class and in the department:

> I think last year I was trying to fit in, I felt more an outsider and trying to work around what the pupils wanted. This year I'm more likely to say you do it my way. If they have an opinion and I have an opinion, mine counts. It makes me sound quite harsh I don't mean it that way. I mean I know why things are going to be like I want them and that's the difference.

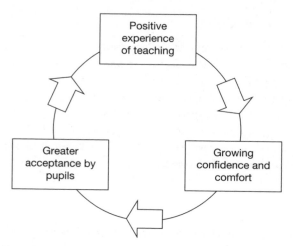

Figure 6.1 Teaching as a virtuous cycle

During the year you might see progress in your teaching as a 'virtuous cycle'. Greater confidence makes you more effective in the classroom and, as your teaching gets better, you sense a greater acceptance and acknowledgement from colleagues and pupils. This, in turn, makes you feel more confident (see Figure 6.1).

While it is easy to see this 'coming together' as something that happens as a matter of course, it is also a consequence of a lot of hard work on your part. You have got where you are through attention to detail in planning, teaching and evaluating your teaching. As Sam, a teacher of modern foreign languages, puts it:

> To give an example, last year I was doing work on expressing opinions, we went through it, set up some practice situations and I thought the kids had got hold of it, but two weeks later it was as if they had never done it before. They needed more activities, more time, I couldn't just lead them through it and say I had taught them. So this year I can see the problems coming. I know how to do it differently. How to do what is in the book, but how to come up with more language work, role plays or more reading and writing, more games which will let them practise what they are learning.

Many explained their teaching was 'taking off' in the second year. They found it easy to sustain their commitment in the face of positive feedback and growing confidence in their own abilities. There was still much to learn but it seemed to be less of a struggle. Like these teachers you may find the second year is one in which you:

- Develop better subject knowledge – you know the schemes of work pupils are working from and you are much better placed to predict the problems pupils might encounter. You are able to answer the questions pupils ask you quickly and confidently.

- Develop better knowledge of your pupils – how best to organise them as a class and as individuals in the class. You might have taught the same individuals over most or all of two years but even if not you will be able to pick up key information about new classes more quickly. You are able to read into colleagues' comments about pupils and see the classroom consequences of reports on difficult pupils and pupils with special needs.

- Are able to much better 'think on your feet'. You are able to use what you know about your pupils to adapt your lesson, for example, to jettison some of what you had planned to do, to spend longer on what they are finding difficult to grasp. You might be able to think up a plenary or a question and answer on the spur of the moment.

- Understand the rhythm of the school year better, for example, when you need to push pupils along to reach key benchmarks and when you need reserves of energy and when you can relax a little.

- Are more assertive in managing classes. You realise, from experience, the importance of setting out explicit rules when you first encounter pupils and are better able to use your voice and presence to convey your authority. You might get the attention of students more easily and set targets during the lesson. You know more about measures to avoid, such as class detentions, and how to emphasise the positive in managing pupil behaviour.

- Have more control of your emotions. You do not get so personally involved when managing pupils and this makes it easier to reflect on what you are doing and reduces the likelihood of confrontation. You might be better placed to understand that it really isn't you that some pupils are angry about: there is much more happening in pupils' lives than you personally can take on or feel responsible for.

- Feel more willing to offer your opinions on teaching and feel more aware of, and more willing to contribute to, the wider role of the school.

With greater self-belief there comes a freeing up: you are less worried about what might happen. For example, Bob found that because he was not preoccupied about pupils' reactions he could gradually stop fearing the worst and focus on his teaching:

> At first when you have a break and even when you know things are alright you come back and you are nervous. You have this fear that you're going to do something wrong. You always look at the worst scenario: what am I going to do if they storm out or don't do what I ask? But it doesn't happen and you start to wonder why you were ever worried in the first place. So I don't have that any more and I am not planning for contingencies any longer. I am going ahead working out what I want to cover and how I want them to work at it.

Bob's example shows the importance of building up classroom routines with pupils. In his case this meant pupils had got used to following simple classroom rules of not speaking when others are talking, of helping each other where appropriate and of generally organising themselves as they go about the classroom. Bob had arrived at a point where he was more relaxed in his teaching, and could create the easy-going relationships with pupils that he had admired in other teachers.

As some of these teachers learnt to become more comfortable in the role of authority in the class they became more focused on the individual needs of pupils and their learning. They were more authoritative and at the same time more 'learner centred'. This theme is developed by Wenda, an art teacher, who explained:

> I am much more in charge of my classroom than when I started here. I tell them what they are learning, what they need to get through, where they are sitting and what they are doing. But I am a much better listener than before and more encouraging, you might say softer. I can stand back, I won't talk about their work until they tell me what they like about it and what they could change. So I start much more from where they are at, helping them to see if there is something they've said which we can work on together, some change they want to make.

Many teachers explained how they understood and were better able to differentiate the various roles expected of them. For example, they could 'put on' being particularly pleased or angry by something an individual had done; they were able to exploit the tone and pitch of their voice better and use silences to get attention. Earlier, the analogy of teaching as acting was used. In their second year many teachers were beginning to 'inhabit the role' and teach in what seemed a more spontaneous and intuitive manner. Some teachers clearly differentiated 'stern' and 'relaxed' roles in their second year of teaching (Hammond 2002). Sara explains:

> I can play within boundaries but in the past I wouldn't. I can talk with students one to one, I am happy to bring down my status and bring it up again when I need to. I have got the confidence to switch between roles. I could come back next week as an authority figure after chilling out with them this week.

Jasbinder makes a similar point:

> I am stricter this year and don't get into the excuses they come up with when they say why they have not done the work. There is much more order in the classroom. So I am stricter, I feel I am able to be stricter but there is also more of me being myself. When I get the chance, say, with the tutor group, or if I am OK with a class I can just switch into being more chatty and friendly with them.

The stern role came with control of behaviour and student learning. In being stern teachers were inflexible and insisted pupils were on task. In being relaxed teachers were much more conversational with pupils, willing to share a joke and more aware of pupils' personal characteristics. This relaxed role was seen more as that of a 'friendly adult'. You might find that both roles are essential to doing and enjoying the job. The stern role was more pronounced when dealing with new classes, challenging classes and younger pupils, and the relaxed one when dealing with more familiar classes and when pupils were more deeply engaged in their work. Many teachers are more likely to be in a relaxed role when taking pupils on trips or working in after-school clubs, but they could also be relaxed in their day-to-day teaching in both one-to-one work and whole-class teaching. In their second year, many teachers said they had learnt how to switch between roles quickly.

Both the stern and relaxed roles were part of the same job of being a teacher. Teachers explained that you could not take on the role of the teacher if you did not know how to be stern. However, they also believed that you could not keep going in teaching if you did not know how to relax and feel spontaneous in the company of the young people you taught. The second year of teaching gives you opportunities to accentuate your stern and relaxed sides. What impact does this have on the pupils you teach?

For you to do

Discuss with a colleague or mentor those aspects of your teaching which have developed and become strengths. If appropriate, collect examples of your work with pupils in a portfolio for later use.

You might feel you are not progressing in the second year

Whereas many teachers describe a 'step change' or qualitative jump in their self-belief and teaching in their second year, this is not true for all. On the positive side you might have 'sailed through' your first year and there might simply be no great jump to take. On the other hand, and more worrying, you might have found the first year particularly challenging, but as the second year gets under way you still see yourself a long way from becoming the confident and able teacher you want to be. If this is the case, there will be a temptation just to get by, to wait for things to sort themselves out. The disadvantage here is loss of job satisfaction and the awareness that you are not reaching the potential you have as a teacher. Try to reflect on your difficulties and address them to the best of your ability. The key lies in *diagnosing* a challenge or problems in your teaching, *identifying* what is causing the difficulty and *generating* solutions to address the difficulty. Some of these solutions, such as smaller class sizes or more resources, are outside your control but there might be others that, while not providing all the answers, will make a difference. By evaluating your solution carefully you will get a better understanding of the problem and identify new challenges. This process of reflection, action and evaluation is sometimes referred to as a reflective learning cycle

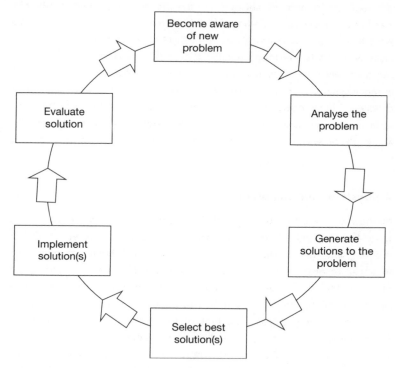

Figure 6.2 A reflective learning cycle to address new problems in your classroom

(see Figure 6.2). An example of such a cycle is illustrated in Mathew's case study below. Addressing problems in teaching is rarely going to be comfortable but it is a necessary process and one made much easier if you have help and support during all steps of the way.

A case study illustrating the reflective learning cycle: classroom management and the second year of teaching

Identification of the problem

Mathew had a satisfactory first year from the point of view of the school but had always found some difficulties with class management and had experiences of abrasive confrontations with some pupils. He was looking forward to finding this side of teaching easier in his second year, but it was not working out. It was galling to have more confrontations with pupils. He found it difficult to talk to colleagues as he could see there were new teachers in the school who seemed to have settled in more quickly than he had and were enjoying better relationships with children. Things came to a head when an incident in his class contributed to the exclusion of one child from school. He could not muddle along, there was a problem of class management he wanted to face up to.

Analysis of the problem

Mathew organised a meeting with his mentor. She tried to put him at ease. She recognised her failure to follow up from last year's CEPD meeting and talked through the classes he had been teaching. She arranged to observe a class. She sat down with Mathew after the lesson and was able to feedback on many strengths in his teaching. She also noticed small but important pointers to some of the tensions he experienced in managing pupils. The first of these considered the transition from whole-class teaching to individual or group work. In the lesson that she had observed the demonstration work had been fine, and question and answer managed well, but Mathew had not been clear enough about what pupils had to do and how long they had to do it. Pace and urgency in the lesson had been lost. Second, she felt Mathew had not been positive enough about pupils' progress at the end of the lesson; he rightly had high expectations of the pupils but was not communicating these expectations in a positive and achievable manner. Third, he was focusing his time and energy on the challenging pupils and almost looking at what could go wrong in the class rather than acknowledging the progress most of the pupils were making and 'strategically ignoring' attention seekers. Mathew found these observations very useful: they put his mind at rest and they focused attention on specific aspects of his teaching that he felt he could address. She also talked with Mathew about his planning of lessons and how well he was catering for the most and least able and whether he was making the lesson accessible to pupils with language difficulties.

Generating solutions

The most important issue Mathew felt he should address was to avoid being sucked into confrontations with attention-seeking pupils. He agreed this was spoiling his relationships with the rest of the class. His mentor advised him not to respond to some interruptions and to stay calm and explain clearly to pupils the consequences of disruptive behaviour for their learning. He was referred to LEA advice on managing classroom behaviour and was advised to observe a colleague, a teacher who had faced similar issues but appeared to be making headway in addressing them. Observing the lesson he saw different strategies for focusing pupils on their work, and how the teacher had a hierarchy of sanctions and would frequently use humour to chivvy pupils before he started admonishing or shouting.

Selecting the best solutions

Mathew felt that there were small but important steps he could take that would help him in managing his classes. First he would plan for clear signposting of stages in the lesson and be as explicit as he knew how in telling pupils the nature of the activity they were expected to carry out and the time scale for completing it. He would remind himself to be positive about pupils' progress in both oral and written feedback to pupils.

Implementation of solutions

Mathew set out to be more positive in his lesson and manage transitions more clearly. He arranged for his HoD to visit his next lesson and used the occasion to go over the 'ground rules' of behaviour with pupils at the start of the lesson. He explained calmly that he wanted everyone to contribute and everyone to succeed but he could not allow some pupils to disrupt the learning of others. He wanted to check that everyone had contracted into this agreement and explained that a sanction for breaching the agreement was to be withdrawn from the classroom and supervised by HoD or other senior teacher. He routinely called on this sanction in the following lessons.

Evaluate

Mathew felt the best guide to evaluating this change in his teaching were his own feelings. He felt less stressed and pupils seemed to be more productive. He monitored how often he had asked pupils to withdraw from the lesson and this decreased over time – another success indicator. It was difficult to make meaningful comparisons but his impression was that pupils' work had improved. He asked his mentor to observe his teaching and she gave him encouraging feedback. However, she referred him back to their conversation about catering for all pupils, particularly the least and most able, in his planning and suggested there were issues in differentiating work that he might want to address. Thus identifying a new problem.

Commentary

This case study shows a teacher addressing a difficulty in his teaching one step at a time. Of course, there are alternative ways of looking at Mathew's difficulty. One cause of his problem might have been a previous lack of support. Another was Mathew's own sensitivity to class management. In his first year, Mathew was often worried over his presence in class and, in his own words, if he was appearing 'strict enough'. He was over compensating and missing opportunities to praise and encourage pupils. One result of this was that pupils were reluctant to tell him when they did not understand what to do. Mathew felt a sense of release by seeking help. He was facing up to a difficulty and he could get another perspective on his teaching and support for his development. A key outcome for Mathew was a renewed confidence that he could do something to improve his relationships with pupils.

If you find yourself in a similar situation to that of Mathew, first try to accept that your second year is still an early stage in your career and there will be limits on your confidence and experience. Mathew had put himself under much more pressure by believing he should not be having problems in class and feeling doubly stressed when they did occur. Second, use any support available to you. Mathew would have benefited if observation arrangements had already been in place. Nonetheless, Mathew did have a nominated mentor who responded well to his concerns and gave him valuable feedback on his teaching.

His mentor was able to help him focus more clearly on pupils and their learning. Third, try to act on any goals or targets you set and get feedback on how well you are meeting them.

A case study illustrating the absence of a reflective learning cycle: stagnation in the second year of teaching

A contrasting scenario to Mathew's is Helen's concern over teaching styles. Helen had settled well into school but felt she was not developing her teaching. As with Mathew, she was putting herself under extra pressure by believing that she should have been a better teacher than she felt herself to be. In her first year everything had been new and she felt she was learning all the time, but in her second year she felt her planning was all routine: introduction, individual work, recapping of main teaching points at the end. Why was this happening? In part, there was less time to plan as she was now teaching a full timetable and had tutor group responsibilities further eating into her preparation time. Another concern was her fear of failure. Last year she felt that as a probationer it was excusable if something she had planned fell flat, but in the second year she was more cautious and felt under more pressure to get it right. She felt her teaching was becoming boring, she was not taking risks and 'she was not feeling very good about it'. She discussed some of these issues with her mentor who reassured Helen of her value to the school, but offered little in the way of concrete advice. In the event Helen staggered through the second year, experimenting now and then with grand gestures, for example role play and non-directed group work, and moved to a new school in her third year.

Commentary

Helen, like Mathew, had identified a problem in her teaching: she wanted to become a more versatile and stimulating teacher. However, she had not analysed the nature of the problem; for example, she had not thought through the opportunities for extending her teaching styles or whether, as things stood, she was meeting her pupils' needs and interests. The school did not help her think through the nature of her concerns. In fact, her mentor barely recognised that she had a problem at all as far as he could see Helen was making good progress and fitting into an appropriate style of teaching. She needed someone with whom she could discuss her dissatisfaction with her teaching and her aspirations as a teacher. A sympathetic colleague could have observed Helen and reassured her of the progress she was making – something that Helen might well have underplayed in her assessment of her own teaching. Without a careful analysis of the problem it was difficult to generate solutions to the stagnation that Helen felt. Perhaps someone from outside her department might have understood her interest in more innovative ways of working, someone who could model approaches such as role play and group work for her and help her become aware of the planning that goes into these styles of working. Helen could then have tried to implement small sustainable changes in her teaching, and adapt them after careful evaluation. Instead, she tried occasional grand gestures that could not be sustained in the face of a demanding timetable and lack of peer support.

Overall, the school did not respond well to Helen's development. Each teacher had a mentor but there were no special arrangements for teachers in their second year or for following up CEPD work. Helen's teaching had not been a cause for concern and her mentor had not made arrangements to talk to her. In the event the only way she felt she could develop her teaching was to move school, though talking to Helen later this seemed something of a shot in the dark.

In a similar situation to Helen's try to be proactive in seeking support. This could be peer support – perhaps there is a close colleague, someone else in their early career, someone in another department with whom you can discuss ideas and plan innovations in your teaching. As discussed in the next chapter you might want to look outside the school to courses or other training events that might help support you in developing your teaching. You might want to look at the possibility of moving school if you feel you are not being encouraged to innovate; again, the pros and cons of doing this are discussed later. You might also look back at Chapter 1 in which we discussed personal values in teaching. Like Helen have you got stuck in a groove in which you are not able to act on your ideas about the ways teachers teach and pupils learn?

Two examples have been described, one showing a reflective learning cycle and one the absence of a reflective learning cycle. The first is very modest in scale but led to significant changes in Mathew's confidence. The second illustrates the difficulties of approaching change in

Box 6.1 Hot-spots in your teaching

Most strategies for professional development focus on generic knowledge and skills, but it is also valuable to focus on specific aspects of the curriculum that you find difficult to teach, and areas that you know pupils have difficulty with. These will differ between subjects. For example, a teacher of modern foreign languages explained difficulties pupils had in grasping the use of the subjunctive tense even after being presented with many examples; an ICT teacher found teaching theoretical aspects of database design difficult; and a PE teacher shied away from gymnastics and invariably ended up organising familiar team games for pupils. If you have a 'hot-spot', an area of the curriculum that is difficult to get over to pupils, try to develop your own reflective learning cycle, analyse the nature of the problem and implement best-fit solutions. You will want to look closely at the obstacles children face; for example, they might have misplaced assumptions about the topic or simply lack appropriate past experience. Perhaps the problem lies in the sheer complexity of what you are teaching, something that is masked in the curriculum material you are using. Addressing a particular difficulty will have important general lessons for your teaching. Try not to ignore hot-spots, work out what is going wrong in your existing approach, talk to children and find out where the problems lie. Once diagnosed get ideas from other teachers and discuss solutions. You will not get it right first time but with feedback you can adapt next time around.

an unsystematic manner. You might want to explore some of these ideas in much more detail, for example through the work of the philosopher John Dewey (1997) and through discussions of action research, an approach based around a cycle of planning, implementing and evaluating. There is an abundance of writing on these topics covering both small- and large-scale projects. One indication of the popularity of these approaches to professional development is that a web search for 'reflective learning' generated 15,000 references; 'action research' generated over a quarter of a million.

For you to do

Use the idea of the reflective learning cycle to address a difficulty in your teaching.

Further observation of other teachers

The focus in so much of your development as a teacher has been on addressing areas of concern. However, you will not want to lose sight of your aspirations as a teacher and inspiring examples of teaching. For example, in writing about effective teaching Turner-Bisset (2001) starts by observing and analysing the work of a teacher she respected. It is an approach you might want to consider in developing your teaching. Take a teacher whose work you admire. Try to describe what happened during a lesson you observed, what impressed you about the lesson and how you felt the teacher brought this about. Here, Natalie describes a PSHE lesson she observed:

> I came in a little late to the class so I had not seen them settled but the first thing that struck you was a sense that they all wanted to be there. The teacher was talking and they were looking at him. If he asked someone a question they were not self-conscious in replying, when he asked a general question he got people wanting to say something. When the class found something funny they laughed in a gentle, not a mocking way. When he saw that he was losing the attention of one of the girls he asked her a direct question and drew her back into the lesson. But when someone else tried to disrupt, later I discovered a lad with a short attention span, both he and the class ignored the interruption and carried on as if nothing had happened.
>
> The lesson was about the use of recreational drugs. The class was brainstorming questions for investigation: who uses drugs? why do they do it? should they be legal? what were the health dangers? what do other countries do? and so on. Pupils volunteered different experiences and opinions. He explained he wanted each group to choose one of the topics and to come up with five or so questions on the topic to investigate. He gave examples of how he thought the investigation might proceed. There were various information packs available and some web addresses to

look at outside of the lesson. They would have a little more time next lesson and then feedback in to the whole group next week – either in the form of a talk, a poster, a role play.

The class divided into groups – later I learnt that they were used to doing this and knew that the teacher would assign pupils to groups if they could not organise themselves quickly and sensibly. He referred to what he called rules for group work but did not spell these out. For the rest of the lesson he came to join different groups, sometimes to monitor what they were saying, sometimes to remind them of group work rules such as listening to all members of the group, sometimes to point out different material they had not looked at. Every now and then he would interrupt the whole class to make a general point, for example to remind them of deadlines for their work and managing tasks within the group. At the end of the lesson each group briefly reported on the progress they had made and on two things they had learnt that lesson. He thanked them for their hard work and reminded them to do any additional preparation for their presentations during the week as they would not have much time next lesson.

What I thought was good about this lesson was the atmosphere in the class – the kids were relaxed but working sensibly at a sensitive topic. They knew and followed rules about group work and really listened to each other and responded to suggestions. I also liked the way pupils could put into practice some of the study skills work they had done on brain storming and handling information.

It's not that easy to say how the teacher brought all this about. One thing that stood out was how well he knew the class, I suspect that things like group work rules have been developed over a long period of time. Another thing was the way he tried to involve everyone – he would really listen to everyone's ideas and make sure other pupils took each idea seriously. He had developed a very collaborative way of working which seemed right considering the topic and the kind of teacher he was. But they were not going to work together until he had set out for them what it was he wanted them to do. He gave the pupils variety, there was something for everyone, talk, reading, a little writing, some whole class work, some group work. Finally he seemed to be aware all the time what was happening in the class. He worked with individual groups but seemed to have an idea what was happening in every group – at least the pupils seemed to think so.

This is not given as a model lesson teaching PSHE; there are perhaps aspects of the lesson you would do differently or you would find inappropriate in your school. But the process Natalie describes is a valuable one, one that you might be familiar with from your training programme but if anything more useful now as you have much more insight into the process of teaching and learning. In her comments Natalie has been able to articulate what she sees as effective teaching and learning (purposeful atmosphere, collaboration, engagement with activities). She has been able to explain how the teacher has brought this effective teaching about (establishing routines, explicit modelling and clear demonstration, monitoring of all pupils, engagement of pupils through relevance and accessibility, variety in planning the lesson, opportunities for learning outside of school and responsiveness to pupils). Following the exercise Natalie can compare her own teaching with that of her colleague. She will not only be able to set new targets for her own teaching but has seen those targets exemplified in the classroom.

For you to do

Carry out an observation of a teacher whose work you admire. What is the teacher doing to make this an effective lesson? Does this lesson illustrate particular standards for teacher assessment in use in your school?

New roles and responsibilities

At the end of the first year you were expected to review your career goals and make plans for addressing any further responsibilities you were going to take on. The extent of these responsibilities will differ depending on the encouragement of the school and how willing and confident you feel about doing something new. The thought of taking on new responsibilities might seem overwhelming at first but if your planning, teaching and assessment have settled into a routine you might have some time and energy for developing your role in school; for example, by taking on a tutor group and having some curriculum responsibilities in your department.

Your tutor group

You will probably be responsible for a tutor group in your second year – though of course you might have already been a tutor in your first year or at least been closely involved with a year group. As a tutor you are expected to be a contact and source of information for all pupils in your tutor group. You have a role in promoting the learning of pupils in your group and will probably be teaching PSHE lessons. For your pupils you are the human face of the school, the one person they see every day. You are there to interpret what is happening in the school and to give them the wider picture of where their school career is heading.

The tutor role is one that many teachers are keen to take on because it gives an opportunity to get to know, and work with, a group over a long time, perhaps to watch individuals grow up, and to develop more informal relationships with a class. There are also considerable spin-offs for your teaching, as Amanda describes:

> As you get to know the group, you learn about the local community, the rivalries inside the school and what they really think of this and that which is going on. You get behind the scenes much more, you see how procedures kick in. Last year if I raised concerns about a child I didn't really know what happened, now you can see who does what and who really follows things through and who doesn't.

Through being a tutor you get to know more about the school and you have the opportunity to work with teachers in other departments. In the longer term, tutoring might open up a career route for you as a head of year. However, taking on a tutor group is a challenge, particularly the first time around, not least because registration of pupils and organisation of such things as parental permission for out of school events cut into your preparation time. In addition you might feel uncomfortable in handling PSHE or other tutorial work if expected to do so. This could be because you have always focused on subject teaching in the past and you might not be comfortable with either the content of tutorial work (e.g. drugs and sex education) or the style in which you are expected to teach.

You might have doubts over other aspects of your role. You might find it difficult to be a good listener, or feel at sea with some of the problems that children describe to you. You might be unsure of your legal responsibilities concerning information that pupils have asked you to keep confidential. You might find the role dominated by having to deal with complaints from other teachers about your group's behaviour in their classes. Most importantly you might be getting mixed messages about tutoring. There is scarcely a school that would not highlight the pastoral side as one of the most important jobs of a teacher and one of the priorities for the school. In reality, you might find that pastoral work is seen as low status by some teachers and you might feel a lack of acknowledgement for doing the job well. In any case constraints on the timetable might mean you lack the time to do what you have been asked to do at anything other than a superficial level.

What can you do? As discussed in the previous chapter your preparation for any new tutor role begins the year before. This will mean observation of other teachers, preferably those who offer good role models for tutorial work, and identifying any courses that would address gaps in your knowledge and experience. You might want to remind yourself of some of the literature you looked at during your training year and, in particular, specialist books on the role of the tutor such as Marland and Rogers (1997), in which the tutor's role in encouraging pupils to take responsibility for their learning is emphasised, and Carnell and Lodge (2000), in which conversations about learning are explored. You might find useful additional resources offered by professional and voluntary organisations – a list of some of these is given in Appendix D. Practical advice is to be organised and methodical in carrying out administrative tasks – easier said than done, but work at it. As in all your teaching, work at the important ground rules – for example, morning registration might be a relaxed time but, if you want punctuality and attention when you have something to say, you will have to work at establishing the same rules as with any other area of your teaching. Whatever feelings you have about the role of tutor, you will need to adopt a positive attitude in front of your class; you are the human face of the school for many of these pupils. You will want to understand the context in which pastoral role is carried out in school and you will benefit from a mentor or guide to your first year, perhaps the head of year. You will meet unexpected situations: perhaps you sense a child is facing some serious difficulties or a child has confided these difficulties to you. Seek advice from your head of year, it is important not to keep things to yourself, there might be other agencies involved. Be careful not to offer confidentiality to a pupil unless you can ensure it; you have a legal and practical obligation to report serious incidents. If you are experiencing difficulty in teaching PSHE be open about it and look for guidance from colleagues. Show you are positive about the role and committed to it; you are seeking help to do it better not moaning about having to do it in the first place.

Focus questions

Review your work as a tutor during your second year.

- What aspects are you happiest about?
- What parts do you want to develop?
- Who or what could be most helpful in supporting your development?

Responsibility within your subject department

The extent of responsibilities taken on by teachers in their early careers differs enormously. Examples ranged from important but low status jobs such as managing equipment through to coordinating transition from Y6 to Y7, designing key stage 3 schemes of work, responsibility for an examination course or introducing new courses and, in some cases, being head or acting head of a small department. In general, most teachers welcomed taking on new responsibilities and felt this developed their confidence and self-esteem. They felt that their career was on track. In many cases, responsibilities were associated with extra salary increments. As seen earlier, the CEPD process involved reflecting on your strengths and how you could draw on these in taking on new roles. In Jo's case this worked out very well:

> I took on responsibility for the key stage 3 schemes. Some part of their thinking, I guess, was we won't give her the exam course to mess up, but it didn't matter. It worked out really well as I could draw on the key stage 3 strategy and bits of it that I believed in. I knew much more about the strategy than people here as it was such a big part of our training plus I knew what was happening in the LEA from my induction meetings. I knew what I

wanted to change in our key stage 3 teaching and this was a great opportunity for me to do something about it.

Many were, not surprisingly, apprehensive about aspects of roles they had taken on, but most enjoyed doing what was asked of them and even those who had taken on leading roles in their department looked back enthusiastically on the challenge. Whatever the role, mentor support with good lines of communication was highly regarded. For example, Bob took over responsibility for an RE department in the second year of school:

> I had a mentor to go to if I needed help. We had a meeting every week, every Thursday after school. And I would go to find him between those meetings if I needed help on something. He was in charge of exam entry to the school and that was the thing that nagged at me, that I would mess up on the entry, and so talking to him lifted a load off my mind. But in every way it just helped to have someone to talk to. He was getting me to think through what I wanted to do and pinning me down on detail, telling me to take it slowly, do it step by step. He never said, 'Don't do this or that', but 'What do you need in terms of resources if you want to change this?' and he let me know about how other people in the school were making changes and who I could talk to.

Not surprisingly, teachers encountered challenges and difficulties in taking on responsibilities. A common one involved introducing changes to a department that was resistant to change. This was something that affected Mary:

> One thing that really upset me this year was being asked to develop more investigative approaches to teaching maths at key stage 3. I spent a lot of time putting these materials together and showing the others how pupils could tackle them. I worked out this assessment scheme too with a self-assessment component. When it came to the meeting it was clear that people didn't want to change. They said they would go along with some of it, I think to spare my feelings, but they weren't doing the self-assessment bit as the pupils could not manage that. I wish I hadn't bothered.

A useful strategy in introducing change into a department is to talk to colleagues one to one before you present them with a scheme of work or an idea for change at a meeting. They will be much more receptive if you can show that you have listened to them and adapted your ideas in line with what they told you. It is far better to get agreement for a small part of your innovation than try to force more ambitious plans that will fall apart. There is a difficult balancing act here between your enthusiasm for change and your knowledge that colleagues have so many other demands made on their time. But if your small innovation works your colleagues will be more receptive to further change in the future. You will also want to talk regularly with your head of department and explain to them what you want to do and why you want to do it. Their support may be needed at a department meeting and they need to be briefed to support you if your ideas are being criticised unproductively.

Sometimes dissatisfaction with a responsibility you have taken on has more to do with the way it has been handed to you rather than the job itself. For example, Sara was asked to introduce a new vocational course in her school, something for which she had not volunteered:

> My role this year has been introducing the new vocational GCSE. I could see no one else wanted to do it so they got me because I was new. It has taken ages of meetings, planning and getting to grips with all the course work and assessment. There are no increment points, you do the job first and then they would see about rewarding you.

In a similar situation you might want to be more determined about your refusal to take on the role or you might want to talk again with senior management about salary enhancement or at least protected time for planning and attending in-service and other courses. However, you might also want to look for opportunities within the job you have been given. For example, Sara's experience of introducing a new course was very valuable and made her ideally placed to apply for better rewarded posts in other schools.

Often being asked to take on too little is a significant cause of dissatisfaction. You might not worry if you want to concentrate on your teaching or the nature of your timetable is changing; for example, you are taking on sixth form work for the first time. However, there are many examples of confident and imaginative teachers who are not being offered roles or, in some cases, are being given low-status or undemanding roles. This usually happens where departmental roles are entrenched and the department puts a low priority on developing a new teacher's career.

High challenge and high support

Many teachers are able to take on further responsibilities in school as the demands of the classroom become less overwhelming. There are good reasons for taking on responsibilities. They can make the job more varied, enhance career rewards and, perhaps most importantly, allow you to implement the changes you want to see take place. There are limits to responsibilities you want to take on and variations in the level of support different teachers find helpful. It is often said that organisations develop most effectively, and individuals feel a greater willingness to innovate and take on responsibilities, with high challenge and high support (see Figure 6.3). In contrast, challenge without the support (trying to do too much without adequate resources) is necessarily stressful and ultimately will lead to 'burn out', resentment or withdrawal. High support and low challenge leaves you little sense of professional fulfilment and may lead to complacency and ultimately boredom. Low challenge and low support can leave you apathetic; the lack of challenge can be depressing and stressful in its own right.

You will want to decide for yourself what are appropriate levels of support and challenge at any particular time. For example, holding down the job of classroom teacher is enough of a challenge for many

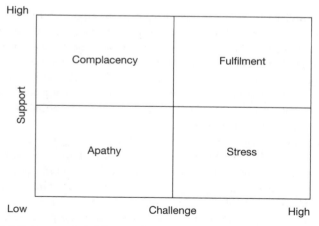

Figure 6.3 Patterns of challenge and support in your career

people in their early career; for others it is not. The challenge you are looking for might be influenced by the demands made on you in the rest of your life. A great many teachers put firm limits on how much they want to take on in school. Judgements about appropriate levels of support are very much in the eye of the beholder. Some teachers will simply want to know that support is there if needed but others will expect a very proactive mentoring process. If support is lacking you might want to consider moving school – something looked at it in more depth in the following chapter.

Focus question

• Reflect on roles or responsibilities you have taken in your department. How, if at all, would you like to develop these and who is best placed to advise you on doing so?

Summary

This chapter has looked at:

• the start of your second year;
• a coming together of knowledge, skills and experience in your teaching;
• addressing areas of concern;
• taking on new roles and responsibilities.

A key message is to try to address difficulties in your teaching at the same time as you look for opportunities to extend your role in school.

Part III

Your career in teaching

Chapter 7

Looking back, looking forward

This book has looked at learning to teach and the early stages of your teaching career. Earlier you were invited to look back on your training programme and your motivation to teach. You considered how your understanding of teaching may have changed and the importance of personal values in teaching. You went on to identify your strengths as a teacher and areas to develop in your teaching. Your concerns were placed in the wider context of reports into initial teacher training and strategies for developing your teaching were discussed. The second section of the book looked at your first two years of teaching and began by considering preparation for the first term and the nature of your induction year. It looked at thriving as well as surviving and went on to describe difficulties you might encounter in the classroom. Strategies for developing your teaching were described and placed in the context of keeping a 'life–work balance'. In Chapter 6 your enhanced status in your second year of teaching, and how you could draw on previous experience in preparing for the start of the new term, were considered. Finally, further areas of concern were reviewed along with new areas of responsibility such as the tutor role and curriculum coordination. You have now had two years in school. In this final section the key messages about learning to teach and your future career in teaching are discussed. Of course much is unpredictable, who knows what might be happening in your personal life let alone your career, but some of the challenges can be signposted. This chapter focuses on your continued development as a teacher and will help you:

- consider key messages in developing your career in teaching;
- appreciate the value of joining a community of practice;
- consider the varied nature of CPD;

- reflect on career routes within teaching;
- consider your continued motivation to teach.

Key messages about teaching

This book has put forward several key messages about teaching and developing your career. These are:

- Your personal values lie at the core of your teaching: adapt them, review them critically but try not to lose sight of them.
- Positive relationships with children lie at the heart of job satisfaction.
- The models of teaching that will appeal most to you tend to match your beliefs about teaching.
- The models of teaching that will appeal most to you address your concerns in teaching your particular classes.
- A key strategy in developing your teaching is to switch focus from you as a teacher to pupils and their learning: this will enable you to better adapt your teaching to their needs and interests.
- There are models and strategies for teaching developed by others which are worth trying but they need to be adapted to your classroom.
- Find time to look at inspirational models of teaching; draw lessons from observing other teachers.
- You have strengths as a teacher, these strengths might provide signposts for developing your teaching and your career.
- You have areas to develop in your teaching: a helpful way to address them is through a reflective learning cycle.
- You will almost inevitably become a more fluent and more confident teacher over time but if you leave this to trial and error progress can be painstakingly slow.
- It is very difficult to develop as a teacher without the help and support of others but . . .
- Support from others may not always be forthcoming. Be proactive in identifying opportunities to develop as a teacher for yourself.
- Excessive commitment to your job may be unhealthy and counterproductive.
- If teaching does not work out there is no rule that says you have to teach.

A fundamental theme underlying all of these messages is that of balance. You are trying to balance your personal view of teaching with the expectations of others – what the sociologists would call the socially constructed view of your role (Berger and Luckmann 1991; Bullough *et al.* 1991). You are balancing your optimism and your self-belief with the realisation that some things are out of your control. You are balancing your commitment to yourself, and to those close to you, with your responsibilities to pupils and colleagues and you are balancing the search for order and routine in the classroom with spontaneity and innovation. None of this is easy to achieve but it is manageable in the longer term if you find yourself in a supportive school, take opportunities for CPD, stay committed to innovation and take advantage of career rewards. These are considered in turn.

What is a supportive school?

A great deal of this book is about how your school – or schools – plays a crucial role in supporting and challenging you to develop your teaching. It is the whole school, the pupils, the colleagues in your department, the support teams, your mentors and your senior management team (SMT) that set the challenge and the support. However, a particular responsibility falls on the SMT (Hammond and Cartwright 2003). Some SMTs give new teachers very limited challenge and support which leaves them feeling unsuccessful and wanting to leave the profession. This is not only bad for the individual teachers concerned but bad for a profession facing difficulties in retention and recruitment. In contrast, there are cases in which the whole school, led by an outstanding SMT, has combined to offer new teachers high challenge and high support. This is clearly shown in considering Julie's experiences, below.

Julie and joining a community of practice

Julie started teacher training on completing her degree. Her training year had gone fairly well. She had enjoyed most of the teaching and felt confident in her planning and her assessment but was aware of weaknesses in her subject knowledge and was not too certain of coping with the class management in her new school, a city comprehensive with low levels of academic attainment. Some of her concerns came out at interview but the school was happy to offer the job based on what they had seen and read about her commitment to teaching and what they saw as her empathy with the goals of the school and knowledge of the community the school served.

The school has an induction tutor who looks after the support and development of all teachers in the school. She arranged for Julie to start her contract in July as a 'super numerary' teacher, just as soon as her training programme had finished. This gave Julie extra time to get to know the department before the start of the new year and the money was very welcome, particularly as she was on the payroll over summer. Julie did some teaching of new topics and received observations of her teaching and got useful feedback. She was given preparation time when she could discuss her new timetable and plan for the year ahead. In one of these meetings the head of department talked through subject knowledge and Julie was encouraged to go to a summer residential course on teaching Shakespeare. The school would pay the cost of the course and in return Julie would report back to the department. Julie made sure that she had all the departmental handbooks and understood the policies. She sketched out schemes of work for next term and prepared her first few lessons. She took four weeks holiday and arranged to meet the head of department again before the start of the new term.

On her first day of the new term each member of the department took it in turns to shadow Julie. They made sure she knew her way to the classrooms in which she was teaching and watched over the corridors as her pupils moved from lesson to lesson. Julie had a contact for each lesson, someone she could turn to immediately in case of any difficulty. Handled wrongly this might have been patronising and intrusive but the support made Julie feel valued in the department. She encountered no outstanding difficulties with her new classes and felt she had moved from trainee to supply teacher to full member of the teaching staff.

Julie settled into a routine. Most of the classes were going more smoothly than she had imagined they would and she was feeling confident. One class was very challenging though. She discussed this with the head of department and looked at possible causes. The head of department freely admitted there were difficult characters in the class and that there was no one, single way of dealing with management difficulties this posed. She asked Julie to focus on individuals: who was causing the difficulties and why? They ran through available support from within pastoral teams. The head of department arranged to observe Julie and made suggestions about the need to be explicit in instructions and following through on sanctions. The feedback reassured Julie and she set action points for teaching this class with dates for follow-up observations. Each term Julie had two more formal interviews with her induction tutor.

Her tutor made sure that Julie was following a training programme and getting release time to go to LEA induction meetings. They discussed various in-service events she might want to attend. In addition to these formal meetings, new teachers met informally both in and out of school and Julie also visited another school to compare notes with a colleague she had trained with.

At the end of the first year Julie was encouraged to talk about her achievements with her tutor. He thanked Julie for her commitment to the school and together they looked at the year ahead. Julie felt a need to consolidate her teaching. She resolved to be clearer about classroom rules at the start of the new term. Together they looked at ways of extending Julie's teaching: her HoD was keen for Julie to do some A level teaching, and they devised a programme of observation and support that would help her.

A programme for career development continued into the second year. This involved more discussion with the induction mentor and target setting. Julie was feeling much more confident in her teaching. One of her goals was to extend her use of drama. Again, she was encouraged to observe other teachers and she was given immediate feedback on her work in class. She had become quite close to other new teachers in the school and organised some peer observations with her colleagues.

At the end of the second year her professional mentor spent a long time discussing her career in the school: Julie was encouraged to take a wider role in the school and they discussed how this would happen. One area that interested her was the support of new teachers and she was co-opted into the support programme for both trainee and new teachers in the school as she had recent experiences to contribute. She explained that she enjoyed the pastoral side to her job and she often talked to sixth form students about her recent experience of university and encouraged them to aim for higher education. A role had come up as assisting the head of sixth form which she was encouraged to take on. The school arranged for her to visit other schools to look into their practice and paid for her to attend a conference organised by a careers advisory service. She worked closely with the head of sixth form who mentored her in her new role. Her programme of support continued into the third year. She felt at the end of the year that she was a very competent classroom teacher and had shown the ability to take on a wider role in school. She was undecided how her career would pan out but had felt a sense of progression in all she had done and looked forward to taking on new roles.

Commentary

Like all new teachers Julie had to address the challenge of settling into the school and of identifying, and addressing, areas for development at the start of her career. She needed to develop her subject knowledge and widen her teaching styles. Later, she became involved in the support of trainee teachers and took on other new roles. These were all considerable challenges but the support was outstanding and worth describing in more detail. Its key features were:

- It was visible to her and to pupils; right from the first day Julie was identified as part of the departmental team, she knew that her colleagues were contactable and made themselves available to help her.
- It provided emotional outlets; she was made to feel at ease in her department and had opportunities to meet other teachers socially.
- It was not confined to a subject department; she was encouraged to meet new teachers in other departments and to work in pastoral teams.
- It was collaborative; members of the department shared ideas and stood up for each other.
- It was explicit; each role Julie took on was carefully explained and demonstrated.
- It was open to criticism; other teachers came forward with ideas but no one claimed to have the right answer.
- It was open to outside influence; Julie was encouraged to visit and learn from other schools and to attend relevant courses.
- It was proactive; Julie was encouraged to set ambitious but attainable career development goals.
- It was sustainable; Julie was encouraged to move from new teacher to full member of teaching teams.

• It had a 'human face'; Julie was encouraged to be positive and her commitment was acknowledged.

Julie had joined a community of practice (Lave and Wenger 1991) which set the kind of challenge and support that got her career off to a flying start. Commentators have long argued whether teaching is a craft to be learnt 'on the job' or an academic discipline with established principles to be explained and then applied (Furlong and Maynard 1995). The weakness of the first approach is that if you are expected to learn on the job what happens if you are working with colleagues who demonstrate inappropriate attitudes (Stones and Morris 1989) or who simply cannot explain what they are doing? You are simply becoming socialised into a community of practitioners not a community of practice. In contrast, if you are given a set of principles without adequate opportunity to try them out you will not know the practical difficulties involved or whether they work for you. A community of practice, as in Julie's school, cuts across the distinction between craft and academic discipline. Teaching is a practical skill but one to be developed through discussion and rigorous analysis.

As you look back on the first stages of your career you might like to reconsider the support you have been offered. If you feel you are working in a community of practice it will be easy to make a long-term commitment to teaching and to a particular school. In contrast, there are some schools which, to be candid, are almost beyond hope and will consistently ignore your development needs. Responsibilities will be landed on you with little consultation, your requests to attend in-service events will be ignored and school based in-service sessions will not face up to the problems within the school. Although many teachers stay in these schools out of commitment to pupils or anxiety about change, there is little that anyone can advise except try to go somewhere else. Between these extremes, perhaps your school has responded to your concerns but has been slow to come forward with offers of support or has encouraged you to set ambitious plans to develop your career. This leaves you looking carefully at the pros and cons of moving school.

Moving school

Mobility between schools in these times of teacher shortages is higher than many people realise. It is not unusual to move school after one or two years and you might well have done so already. If not, why consider a move now? Leaving aside the ending of a short-term contract there might be issues that are *pushing* you away from your present school. Perhaps your first school was something of a compromise. You were offered a job and did not want to wait to see if something more suitable came along. It is not really the right school for you. You might be looking for somewhere more challenging, less challenging, more innovative, more traditional, a wider or narrower age range or whatever. Perhaps the school did not match your image, it is less innovative or less organised than you had thought; perhaps the children are not really the types of children you wanted to work with. Your dissatisfaction might extend to specific aspects of the support and encouragement you have had at school. You might have settled in well at the school but you have not developed your teaching in the way you had hoped. You were not given the support and mentoring you had hoped for in the first year and there are very restricted opportunities for in-service training and other support. You are not being pushed to develop your teaching. There might be very restricted career opportunities; for example, there is very limited mobility because everyone has their role which they hang on to. You are looking to be head of department and you want to get on. Very often teachers feel that heads of department or senior management are pushing them away from a school. Some teachers spoke of managers who were overly bureaucratic, insensitive and 'fussy'.

As well as feeling pushed away from a school you might feel *pulled* towards a new school. The school might fit your personal ethos better, there is a responsibility associated with the post you want to take on and there is an opportunity to develop your teaching in a sympathetic setting. You might see an advantage in getting another perspective on teaching, perhaps you can pick and choose best features from teaching styles you have seen in two different schools. You might find it attractive to work in a bigger department or a school that offers more support. You might simply be attracted to the idea of making a clean start – an empty pigeon hole, a clean desk, colleagues and pupils with no preconceptions about you or your teaching.

Most teachers who had moved school talked in an overwhelmingly positive way about their experiences. But this does not add up to a blanket recommendation to move. Those who moved were feeling restricted or unhappy where they were and the very act of moving might well have given them a 'kick start' and made them feel more in control over their career.

Many teachers paid much more attention to what was pushing them away rather than what was pulling them to a new school (e.g. Hammond and Cartwright 2003 and, more generally, Herzberg 1971) and perhaps some will, in time, find the same causes of dissatisfaction in their new schools. If you are thinking of applying for a post elsewhere, investigate the school thoroughly. You might be able to draw on colleagues you have met at LEA or in-service events to find out more. Make sure you are aware of any major changes ahead; for example new courses being offered, an impending bid for specialist status, a new head of department. You might want to look at recent OFSTED reports (the web address is given in Appendix C) but remember judgements about the school could be quite dated, or the controversial performance tables for the school published by the DfES(www.dfes.gov.uk/performancetables). Look at interview advice given in Appendix A – you will be expected to have a fuller portfolio of work on which to draw and be better able to back up your answers with classroom experiences. If you are asked why you want to leave your present school focus on the attractions of the new school: 'I feel confident of becoming a better teacher here' leaves a more positive impression than focusing on the shortcomings of your present school.

Teachers who moved schools found there was a settling-in period that involved some of the disorientation and testing they experienced in their first year. But most were quick to settle and found they could draw on their subject knowledge even if teaching to different schemes of work. They found much in their teaching style that was transferable, as Paul explains:

> When I started here, it was hard at first as I had to set out where I stood from scratch. But when I was not happy with the classes I 'barked' at them and got pretty much the same reaction here as my previous school. They went quiet and they settled down and got on with it. I was expecting much bigger differences than I encountered. Looking back it was not such a big jump.

In contrast, Ben moved to a much more challenging school and found it took much longer to settle in, but he was still glad to have moved:

> Yes it has been hard. There are kids here who frankly I can't deal with. They don't respond in the same way. Perhaps you may have had one or two of these personalities last year but this year it is

four or five at least who don't want to be there who are pushing
you all the time. It has not been easy and sometimes I have gone
home feeling like a beginner again. But I remind myself of why
I left and I know it was the right choice, the teaching will get
better I know but the management and the bullying in my last
school wasn't going to change and that is something I could not
put up with.

Should you consider moving school in your early career? There is no
hard and fast answer. You will want to weigh the opportunities
in your present school against those being offered elsewhere and the
advantage of knowing pupils and colleagues where you are against the
attraction of working from a clean slate. Getting another perspective
on teaching is going to help but your school might already be
giving you opportunities to visit and collaborate with teachers in other
schools in any case. If you are unhappy where you are then reaching a
decision to move will be easier, but ask yourself if your new school will
really address what has unsettled you. It might seem an obvious point
but if your concern is over your career development there would be little to gain in the long run if you chose to go somewhere else simply
because the exam results are better. Alternatively, you might be
attracted to another school because it involves a promotion but if the
school is beset by low morale and high staff turnover, think again. If
your concern is with the culture of your present school you might, like
Ben, want to go somewhere that is more challenging but also more
supportive.

Focus questions

- How would you characterise the level of support and challenge you have experienced in your school?
- Can you identify ways in which you would like your career
  to develop?
- What kind of support would be of most benefit to you? Is
  this school going to help you develop your long-term career?

Your continuing professional development (CPD)

Teachers often see CPD in terms of the courses they attend and the training days that the school organises, but it is a much broader concept and CPD can be used to describe anything that develops your skills, knowledge and understanding of teaching and learning. CPD covers both formal courses, meetings, working parties and the informal reflections and conversations you have about teaching as well as any reading you do about your job.

As described throughout this book, one, if not the most important, resource you have for supporting your CPD is your department and your school and this will continue to be the case. You will need to maintain your curiosity about colleagues' teaching. Using sufficient tact and diplomacy, ask for advice on your teaching, seek other teachers' comments on your ideas. Share your planning with a colleague who is teaching the same course as you; ask to observe a lesson and show that you can keep your evaluation confidential. Resist opportunities to be negative about other colleagues. Think back to the kind of school-based activities you carried out during your training programme such as shadowing pupils: can these be helpful now?

If your school is not offering the right levels of support, are there opportunities to change the culture of the school from below, for example, by organising your own co-mentoring? The trick here is to find a person or people with whom you get on well and who will be honest and open with you and will want you to be honest and open in return. Of course, this is very difficult given how very little non-contact time you have and you might find other teachers initially reluctant to work with you. But the importance of observation for developing teaching is increasingly accepted and some teachers have been very successful in developing peer support of this kind. One place to start is observation of each other's teaching – with the observer giving feedback followed by a discussion of strengths and areas to develop. Look for opportunities to share development goals. You might both have set yourself targets to introduce more group work into your teaching; can you compare plans and report back on how you got on? You might have concerns over your written feedback to pupils; compare these with a colleague, are there ideas you can take to develop your teaching?

You might have increasing opportunities to reflect on teaching and learning in your department by contributing to the training of student teachers or newly qualified teachers. You might not have full responsibility for this but show you are interested and want to get involved. In the case of student teachers, make clear you are not looking for someone to take your class while you disappear: you want to help and put something back. There are some risks in terms of disruption to the class, as you will know from your own training, but you will learn a lot by watching a beginner. As seen in earlier chapters, sometimes you need to observe a flawed performance to understand the skills of a practised performer and you will learn even more by offering to coach the beginner teacher. If you can extend your involvement you might find mentoring gives you opportunities to attend training events as well as to meet other teachers within the training partnership.

Be proactive in identifying roles in the department you might like to take on. Reflect on what you would most like to change and what you are best placed to carry out. Be open about your uncertainties and specific about the support you would like in order to do the job. You will have to draw your own conclusions on the scale points or other rewards or compensations you expect. Keep an eye out for whole-school initiatives, for example, special projects such as after-school clubs, research into boys' achievement, ethnic minority provision. You might go further and apply for an internal post of responsibility in the school. You will be very reluctant to apply for these posts if no one has suggested to you to do so and you might feel embarrassed if you are rejected, but at the least find out what the school is looking for, get advice on how you can prepare for the post and, unless the odds really are stacked against you, apply. If unsuccessful, get feedback on how you presented yourself and why you did not get the job.

In-service events

Schools will from time to time run their own in-service events either at a departmental or school level. If other colleagues are running an event, help by letting them know which topics you would find most useful to be covered. Ask to attend external training events. These have the obvious advantage of allowing you to compare experiences in different schools often going well beyond the stated aims of the event. A disadvantage of outside training is a loss of focus on your own school and pupils.

On the positive side many teachers say, not surprisingly, that they found events that addressed the issues they faced with their classes were the most valuable, particularly when these were led by people who 'radiated' experience and expertise. Follow-up sessions were useful as they gave an impetus to at least try out a new approach in the classroom because teachers knew they were going to meet again to share experiences. Some providers build in peer observation sessions, another strong motivation to innovate and an excellent opportunity for feedback. Teachers wanted to make choices in their CPD activities and acknowledgement of what they already knew; for example, one teacher spoke about the value of her own individualised training programme throughout her early career.

Teachers spoke about difficulties of attending sessions out of school. The obvious difficulty was one of cost to the school – not so much of the course but the expense of supply cover. However, teachers themselves were often reluctant to apply for courses because it would involve missing lessons they were scheduled to teach and might impose extra work on colleagues in supervising cover arrangements. They saw the benefits of school-based in-service training but were critical of the standard of professionalism of colleagues leading sessions.

There are mixed messages here. There are bound to be some very poor training providers and some sessions that miss the mark, but there is a responsibility on you to get the most out of your training. This means making your own suggestions as to what you would like your department to work on and, if appropriate, suggesting some aspect of your teaching you would like to share with other people. If you are going out of school, explain your training needs to the in-service provider. Make clear that you want to come away with something you can use in your classroom. Some key questions to ask about any training event are: what is it about; what ideas can I take from it; what will help me in implementing this idea; what will constrain me and how can I get round it; how can I evaluate the idea and how can I inform other people?

In any training there is a balance between the short-term cost to you, your pupils and your colleagues and the long-term benefit of getting access to a resource which could make a difference to your teaching. You and your school cannot always let short-term considerations stop you from going to events – though this is easier said than done particularly if you do not work in a harmonious and supportive department.

Focus question

- Can you identify any in-service training events which might help you to develop your teaching?

Other sources of in-service support

In addition to in-service events there are many organisations and people that can further your development as a teacher. The extent of online help has mushroomed in recent years. The National Grid for Learning (see Appendix C) gives you access to materials, news and discussion while many LEAs seem well advanced in developing grids for learning more attuned to local needs. Subject associations are an invaluable source of information and a good way to make contact with other teachers and contribute to the development of your subject. Nearly all subject associations organise conferences and provide curriculum advice. A list of some of the major associations is given in Appendix D along with names of other organisations that support teachers and teaching. There are many more, which a little web exploration will turn up.

There are other ways of sharing ideas with teachers from nearby schools. Look out for any formal or informal links your school has had with Beacon schools or schools involved in the DfES Leading Edge Partnership Programme (see Appendix B) or with other schools with good reputations for aspects of their work. If there are no formal links, see if it is feasible to organise your own visit to a Beacon school and, if you are in one, offer to contribute to any programmes or support they offer.

Local education authorities often organise networks of teachers interested in particular topics: contact local advisory services to find out more. The Teacher Training Agency has supported some regional networks, you can find out more on the TTA web site. You might want to look back at the Fast Track Programme as a more targeted form of career development. This programme has been associated with initial teacher training but you can apply to enter it later in your career. You need to demonstrate a 'high standard of performance, need to have ambition and a strong commitment to school improvement'. Information for serving teachers who wish to join the Fast Track Programme can be found at the DfES web site – see Appendix B.

Professional development programmes and higher degrees

LEAs often offer programmes of training or support for small-scale research. You may also find details of postgraduate professional development programmes through the LEA. These are generally short courses which are heavily supported by the TTA. It is estimated that some 25,000 teachers were involved in the previous award-bearing scheme in any one year (Soulsby and Swain 2003). These programmes allow you to accumulate credits and put them towards a higher degree qualification. Alternatively, you might be interested in working towards a full qualification course right away at a local higher education institution. These courses lead to certificates, diplomas or higher degrees such as a Master of Educational Studies (M.Ed.), Master of Philosophy (M.Phil.) or Doctorate (Ph.D. or Ed.D.). You can find out about courses through The Higher Education and Research Opportunities in the UK web site (www.hero.ac.uk) or simply ask at your local institution or look at advertisements in the educational press. You will find opportunities for both distance learning (the Open University is a major provider here but look at local providers too) and face-to-face courses.

There are any number of reasons why you might want to start studying for a research degree, but one of the most common is simply intellectual curiosity about the ideas and principles underlying your teaching. To take one example, a lot of importance has been given in recent years to learning styles, and the idea of there being visual, kinaesthetic and auditory types of learner (Smith 1996). Much of this work has been very valuable for teachers, illustrated, for example, by Corrine's lesson planning in Chapter 2. The idea of categorising learning styles highlights the diversity inside a classroom and the importance of making learning accessible to all. It is an easily understood concept which, once grasped and implemented, helps you develop your teaching quite markedly. At the same time you might well have formed the view that simply categorising learning styles does not add up to a 'proper' theory of teaching and learning. Learning styles are more to do with the 'tactics' which we as learners may use, rather than the much wider issue of how we grasp and assimilate new ideas in the first place. The bigger theories are ones such as behaviourism, constructivism and social constructivism (Desforges 1995) and, at some level at least, these underlie nearly all of your teaching. For example, some of the ideas on behaviour management discussed earlier draw on the behaviourist idea that learning is reinforced by positive feedback. While social constructivism, with its idea that learning is social and involves dialogue and support from a more experienced guide, informs some of the key stage 3 strategy material on, say, questioning, explanation and group work (DfES 2003b) discussed earlier. Understanding these theories in greater depth might well make you an extended teacher – one who is able to articulate and evaluate what you are doing in the classroom and explain to others why you are doing it.

A second motivation to undertake further academic study is that this could help you find practical ways to better support pupils' learning. It can do this by giving you access to other models of teaching and pointing you to a knowledge base on which to make judgements. To take one example almost at random: a review (Hallam 2004) of research on homework reported that homework makes only a relatively small contribution to performance on achievement tests. Some of the difficulties lie in the lack of support, or rather lack of appropriate support, pupils get at home; hence the review argues the case for homework to be done in out-of-hours homework clubs rather than at home. Studies like this help as they often confirm your own experiences as a teacher while pointing to practical ways forward which you, or in this case your school, might investigate. They cannot tell you what you should do, but they raise issues and help you predict the likely impact of an innovation. Many higher education courses go further than this and support you through the implementation and evaluation of an innovation in your teaching or in your school through carrying out an action research project. Such a project may cover developments in more or less any aspect of teaching and learning; for example, formative assessment, role play in history teaching, the contribution of ICT to teaching data handling, the impact of the literacy strategy, introducing the new vocational curriculum, the role of pupil talk in learning algebra, the impact of citizenship on teaching PSHE, the value of exchange visits in learning languages, positive attitudes to behaviour management and so on.

Many teachers talked positively about the post-degree courses they had followed and spoke enthusiastically about the in-depth studies they had carried out. However, such courses only appealed to a minority of teachers and some were very sceptical about their value (Shaw and Hammond 2003). They felt these courses would be too academic, too time consuming and remote from their concerns. Some also raised concerns about the usefulness of the research literature and you might want to look at critical comments by Tooley (1998) and responses including those of Gorard and Taylor (2003).

Any course involves a high input of time and sometimes money. On the first issue, try to talk to colleagues who have taken similar courses in the past and then talk to course tutors. Explain what you want out of the course and see if it suits you and, just as important, that you are fully aware of the commitment it requires. Look at some of the texts used within the course. There is a very large research literature and an edited collection such as Leach and Moon (1999) and Banks and Mayes (2001) will give you a flavour of some of the issues that might be discussed within a course dealing with the early professional development of teachers. Look at some of the action research literature (e.g. McNiff *et al.* 1996) if the course claims to offer opportunities for 'practitioner research'.

Regarding costs, some schools or LEAs will be able to offer limited support for you and some higher education institutions will lower costs if you work in a partnership school. Support from school is much more likely to be forthcoming if you can explain how attending the course will impact on your teaching and on the school as a whole. For example, explain how your research project on multiple intelligences will lead to innovation in your department and offer to run in-service sessions on your work for other teachers. The DfES has, at times, run schemes to support teachers' CPD. A Professional Bursaries Scheme was introduced which entitled teachers to a £500 bursary in both their fourth and fifth years of teaching to spend on professional development, but you will need to get an update on this or any other schemes from the DfES CPD web site (see Appendix C). Occasionally there are other opportunities of support from trusts and charitable organisations which you can find out about from your professional association, LEA or local university.

You can get a wider perspective on educational research through the British Educational Research Association (BERA) and networks such as the Collaborative Action Research Network (CARN). Your subject association is your first port of call for subject-related matters. You might want to look further afield for CPD opportunities. Advice on European Union-funded initiatives is available from the Central Bureau, which is part of the British Council. For details of the organisations, see Appendix C.

Focus questions

- Discuss your future career with a relevant member of senior management. How would you most like to see your career develop? How can you best prepare for this?

Commitment to continual innovation in teaching

Taking on academic study is part of the wider question about the extent to which it is practical or even desirable to reflect on your teaching. You will set your own limits on this and your willingness to make changes based on your reflections. You might be quite content to follow the schemes of work given to you and stay close to a tried and trusted approach to planning, teaching and assessment. In contrast, for some people innovation and change is second nature, it keeps them 'on their toes' and motivated. There is a balance here to be made in terms of cost and benefit. If you extend yourself by trying new teaching styles, you will develop a wider repertoire and be more able to adapt to different types of learners. You will be able to make considered choices about your teaching. However, there is a short-term cost to innovation. In your first attempts you might be hesitant, you might unsettle pupils used to your way of working, you might be reminded, if only for a moment, how you felt when you first started teaching. You might be investing reserves of time and energy that are in short supply. You might experience 'diminishing returns' on your efforts and feel that you are tapping only at the margins of your development as a teacher.

However, there are very good reasons to look at what you do with a fresh pair of eyes – what the management gurus might call 'thinking outside the box'. You might have become much better at one way of working but now take the limitations within that approach very much for granted. For example, through a painful period of trial and error, you might have developed routines for whole-class discussions that work. You are clear, your pupils are well ordered, but you might be asking the same kinds of questions and the same people are responding to them. From your point of view, you have become a confident and able teacher, and no one is saying you have not. However, there are limitations and it might be worthwhile investigating, say, ways of using questioning to involve all pupils or to think up new strategies to involve those who feel uneasy contributing in front of other people. Taking a fresh look at your teaching is a way of updating your professional skills and avoiding going stale. Below, we look at two examples of teachers for whom small innovations led to a quite fundamental shift in their approach to teaching. The first looks at the use of ICT, something initially discussed in Chapter 1.

Using ICT in subject teaching

Sally is a geography teacher in her third year of teaching. Her school had invested heavily in computer facilities and had put on some introductory sessions on using computers for teachers. These did not grab the attention of many in the school but Sally saw something in the use of the internet that interested her. Teachers were encouraged to try out ICT in their lessons and Sally focused on the use of the internet within the project work pupils were carrying out. She saw several attractions. Pupils seemed generally interested in using ICT and were doing so increasingly on their own initiative. She felt the sites she had seen were more visual and more up to date than any of the text books they were using. But why bother to change? She was very satisfied with the classes she was teaching, no one else in her department seemed particularly bothered about using computers and she risked upsetting the relationships she had with pupils by trying something new. However, she decided to hang on to the idea of introducing ICT as she felt that it gave her opportunities to make her teaching more exploratory. For example, there were so many resources over the world wide web that pupils would have to make their own decisions on what to look at and where to follow up links.

The ICT room was booked for a series of sessions with her Y9 pupils. She felt confident in her use of the equipment but had the support of an ICT technician in case things went wrong. She made her own evaluations of the lessons and organised some peer observations with a colleague who was carrying out a similar innovation in another department. She felt the pupils responded really well to using ICT and, in particular, the more challenging pupils seemed more 'on task'. The best work was of a very high standard: it looked more professional, it had incorporated relevant images and references to events were up to date. On the debit side she felt there had been too much 'playing around'; some pupils were flicking from site to site looking for the most appealing images, there was too much cutting and pasting of text into final reports and too little thought about the quality and reliability of sources. Overall, she felt there was enough in the use of ICT to make it worthwhile continuing with another project but she was going to make changes. She developed a more directed style of working – she set tasks around certain web sites she had selected and explained much more clearly how she wanted pupils to write reports. She modelled what they had to do. Her review of pupils' work was now much more positive. She went on to make much more use of ICT and developed a site of materials for pupils to access out of school.

Commentary

The scenario illustrates a teacher who made a quite radical move from not using ICT to someone who considered the use of ICT in her planning as second nature. This came about because she could see that the use of ICT was strategically important for the school. However, she could become committed to the use of ICT only when she developed her own thoughts on which programmes to use and settled into a preferred teaching style. Her initial idea was that ICT would allow a more learner-centred approach. In fact, she backtracked a little from this stance but it did not matter, it gave her the motivation to get started. She was further encouraged as she felt that pupils would respond well to using computers and, very largely, they did. Evaluation was important in the project; in particular, she had found it valuable to pair up and discuss experiences with a colleague. This enabled her to get other perspectives and later to refine her project.

Rethinking support for disaffected pupils

This case study concerns Shaun, a teacher of history who was considering moving jobs. The school responded quickly, they did not want to lose him and offered him a salary increment if he would take on a project they had been considering on motivation of low achievers in Y11. Pupils of very different abilities, attitudes and backgrounds attended the school including a noticeable group of disaffected pupils who were low-attaining and causing disciplinary problems in several classes. He realised this was going to be a challenging project and one concerning an issue he had not thought deeply about. But there were attractions. It was an additional responsibility, it brought another salary increment and it would provide some variety in his job. He was given time within a new timetable to support teachers or run further sessions with pupils.

He decided to refocus the project on low achievers rather than under-achievement or behaviour management per se, though the two had become closely bound together in the minds of most teachers he spoke to. He identified a group of pupils to monitor and support. He put together profiles of these pupils, and tracked their progress and behaviour in lessons. He interviewed the pupils and the teachers who taught them. He found that pupils had a very low threshold for learning new material before feelings of frustration and exclusion took over. The teachers addressed this by 'preparing for containment'; for example, getting pupils to complete a wordsearch or simple worksheet, something he knew from his own experience.

He tried to take a fresh look at teaching these pupils. One problem was that lessons were invariably based on text exercises, which pupils found repetitive and boring. He and his colleagues would need to provide greater variety in lessons and activities that were more adventurous but carefully targeted. They would need to be more sensitive to language difficulties. He developed and supported a study skills programme including the use of mind-mapping activities to help pupils organise their thoughts on a topic. Responding to pupils' suggestions he developed some group-work scenarios and role plays. He explained some of this work to his colleagues and asked if he could support them by helping to introduce new approaches in their lessons. He evaluated the results of the project at half-term intervals using interviews with teachers, with pupils and through school data such as truancy and attendance. Some aspects of the support programme fell flat but overall the results were impressive, though he was honest enough to say that they were almost bound to be because pupils were being supported with extra help. There was a considerable spin-off in the rest of his teaching. He routinely prepared for variety in his lessons and paid much closer attention to supporting pupils in their language difficulties. He became a very different teacher to the one he started the year as.

Commentary

Shaun's scenario differs from Sally's because he was specifically asked by the school to take on a formal responsibility within the school. He was being asked to take a fresh look both at his role in school and his approach to teaching. When it came to innovation within teaching, Shaun, like Sally, needed to find his own stance on an innovation, in his case to redefine the target group for the project and to develop a pupil-centred solution. Like Sally, Shaun took pains to evaluate his work – something that obviously had to be done in a collaborative manner as he was working with other teachers. Again like Sally, what had started as quite a small innovation led to a significant change in how he planned his teaching.

Both Shaun's and Sally's projects involved a lot more detailed planning and work than can be considered here, but together they provide lessons for thinking about new approaches to teaching. First, be strategic, pick on something that will get the interest or, better, the active support of the school. Second, ask yourself if it is something that will get a positive response from at least some of the pupils. Third, find your own personal angle on the innovation – there is no point in doing it otherwise. Fourth, build in some evaluation of your work. Fifth, look to collaborate with a colleague if only to compare notes. Sixth, think big but start small: recall the cyclical nature of reflective learning discussed in a previous chapter. Small steps may lead to more fundamental changes. You might compare these points with Fullan's very influential account of managing change in schools (2001).

For you to do

Are there new approaches to teaching which you have seen or read about that appeal to you? Investigate these approaches further and develop innovations, small steps at first, in your teaching. Seek feedback from pupils and colleagues and consider ways of taking these innovations forward.

How do I keep a life–work balance?

The difficulties of excessive demands were discussed in Chapter 2 but this is something that will not go away. It is a general issue with both employers and trade unions becoming increasingly concerned about the long hours that people in the UK are working. The concern is not simply about an individual's quality of life but also the impact on any organisation if the people within it are stressed and over-tired. Teachers are particularly vulnerable to excessive hours. The job really is undoable in the time you have, if you cut corners you feel as if you are letting some children down. In a recent survey (Smithers and Robinson 2003) five main factors were found to influence teachers' decisions to leave teaching: workload, new challenge, the school situation, salary and personal circumstances. Of these, workload was by far the most important, and salary the least.

As discussed in Chapter 1, teachers' concerns about workload are very often focused on the nature of the task rather than the hours allotted to it. For example, a new teacher, Sammy, explained how she had spent the weekend helping in a sponsored orienteering activity for pupils. To her this did not seem an unreasonable encroachment on her free time. It was something she volunteered to do and enjoyed doing. You can easily think of times in your early career when it will have seemed effortless to dedicate time and effort in planning a new course, assist a pupil with difficulties after school or take part in a voluntary activity. In contrast, like Sammy, you will be able to describe other tasks which were tedious, bureaucratic and seemed to make very little contribution to the work of the school. Another teacher, Shaheed, focused on two examples in respect of voluntary activities he had taken part in:

> First, we organised an after-school club. We got £2,000 for running it which was fine. I wrote the bid and I put in extra time after school to run it. It was a good thing and a good thing for the school to be involved with. Then we had to write a 2,000-word report on our targets and outcomes. I really didn't mind the extra time I put in and I didn't mind that we couldn't use the money for staff time but when it came to the report, that did it for me. Don't get me wrong, they can come in and see what we did was all above board but why should I have to write a report, who was going to look at it and why this long? The second example is going on a residential trip. Again, all voluntary and you are responsible for the children 24 hours a day, but to do the trip you have to answer 44 risk assessment questions. It took hours to sort out. It is things like this which are sucking the life out of the job.

There is no easy solution to Shaheed's concerns about account-ability. These and other procedures are part of the culture in which public services operate and, to some extent, have to operate. But schools have found themselves held particularly to account. This has led to excessive, sometimes obsessive, documentation. This is some-thing of a paradox given that teaching is a profession in which there is always going to be some uncertainty over the best way to do the job and how you measure the impact you are having on pupils. As Max describes:

> In my school there are filing cabinets full of examples of children's work that we have collected and copied and filed. All this to show the next inspection team evidence of how we moderate and assess work and how we grade pupils and, of course, how good we are. It has taken hours and I could talk about the hours we have put into the course booklets, reports and other paperwork as well. None of this makes us better teachers. It simply takes up our time and effort. I didn't go into teaching for this.

Again, no easy solution. You are being asked to be accountable and to show you are raising standards when, very often, you are faced with insufficient resources and a lack of parental support for very difficult pupils. If you are worried about the hours you are working, refer back to earlier advice. In particular, talk to colleagues and try to focus on the aspects of your work that seem most burdensome. For example, you might have to put less time and effort into marking and report writing, you might be able to use ICT more for repetitive writing tasks and self-assessment and peer assessment might lessen the marking load. There might be ways in which you can collaborate with other teachers; for example, sharing the preparation of materials for the same course. There is an irony here that developing a collaborative response to prioritising and sharing workloads requires a detached view of the problem, a willingness to explore new angles and to take risks in devel-oping new ways of working. Yet, if you are feeling overstretched, time and detachment are in short supply. It will nearly always seem easier to continue with existing routines and 'fire fighting' crises every now and then. To tackle workloads seriously your department will need to mark off non-contact time to discuss the issue and develop practical proposals. There are no one-off solutions, but schools can do some-thing about workloads if they take the problem seriously and are able or prepared to invest in support staff. If your school is not addressing workloads, compare experiences with colleagues. Do you have common concerns that should be raised with senior management or that you would like raised by your trade union or staff association? Some senior management teams will feel threatened by a discussion of workloads but keep in mind the positive nature of your goals. You are equally committed to your school, manageable workloads are in everyone's interest.

Some approaches to addressing unsustainable workloads might have uncomfortable implications for how well you feel you are doing your job, but here it is a question of priorities. You need to have some time and energy left over for new responsibilities such as mentoring or pastoral work. Be strategic about how you invest your time. This means difficult choices. For example, should you put time and energy into developing a new vocational course or should you be overhauling your teaching of the existing GCSE course? It might have to be one or the other, not both. There are limits on your time: try to block free time for yourself and find commitment and interests outside of teaching. Exceptional commitment to teaching is rightly praised but teaching should not require special sacrifices. You are asked to do the best you can with the time, materials and resources available.

The issue of teacher workloads has been taken up through an agreement negotiated between the DfES and most of the teacher and other interested unions (DfES 2002b, 2003b and see specialist press for regular updates, e.g. *Guardian Education* 2004). This agreement aims to achieve progressive reductions in teachers' overall hours through ensuring that teachers do not routinely undertake administrative and clerical tasks; have a reasonable work–life balance; have a reduced burden of cover for absent colleagues; have guaranteed planning, preparation and assessment time within the school day, to support their teaching, individually and collaboratively; and have a reasonable allocation of time in support of their leadership and management responsibilities. The agreement also calls for reductions in paperwork and bureaucracy. It is envisaged that schools will employ more support staff and use support staff in extended roles, including personal administrative assistants for teachers, additional technical support, cover supervisors and high-level teaching assistants. Such an extension of the role of support staff has obvious implications for training and salaries.

The agreement seems more radical than it first appears. For example, teachers will need to make the decisions on most of the administrative and academic-related tasks for which they will be offered support. They might well find it easier to finish the work for themselves rather than explain the detail of what they want and how they want to do it. However, the importance of the agreement is that it raises the profile of workloads in teaching and provides a focus and impetus to tackling excessive hours both at departmental and school level. Two tasks that most teachers would like to see taken away from them are covering for absent teachers and the invigilation of exam classes. Much here will depend on available resources and strength of feeling. The DfES has also recommended that ICT could make a contribution to reducing workload; for example, through keeping standard templates of letters and reports (Price Waterhouse 2001). There are long-term benefits but do not underestimate the short-term cost of designing and implementing ICT solutions.

Focus questions

- How are workload issues being addressed in your school?
- Do you have particular concerns about your workload which are not being addressed?

Career rewards

A further element in your career development concerns the material rewards. The financial reward from teaching cannot, in itself, provide you with job satisfaction or motivation to teach, but lack of reward can leave you dissatisfied about the way your career is heading and what your school is asking of you. Of course, there is a wider context here and you might want to raise general issues about teacher pay and conditions with your union or professional association. However, this does not prevent you from considering your own personal circumstances. One concern you might have is the process of threshold payments. This might appear some way off but it gives you an indication of the kinds of schemes popular with governments and how career rewards are likely to be 'performance driven'.

The aim behind threshold payments is that after a certain point pay increment awards are not automatic. You have to, as you may well have guessed, reach a set of standards which, at the time of writing, cover knowledge and understanding; teaching and assessment; pupil progress, wider professional effectiveness; and professional characteristics. Application is entirely voluntary and likely to be a one-off exercise. Threshold takes you onto a new upper pay scale (see the DfES site for up-to-date details). Teachers have found the threshold process time consuming but made much easier if they have been collecting a portfolio of evidence. This portfolio contains examples of your work with pupils and is something you can get in the habit of updating throughout your career. As you reach threshold, talk to others who have gone through the process and seek advice from your trade union. Your head's comments are an essential part of the process (insight into the process from a teacher's perspective is provided by Gilbert 2004). Being refused threshold, or refused further transitions within the threshold scale, can be difficult to accept. If you are in this position, get detailed feedback on what you can do to fulfil the requirements. Speak to your union representative if you feel you have been treated unfairly.

Another type of enhanced pay scale is offered through the Advanced Skills Teacher route. The Advanced Skills Teacher (AST) programme is designed to offer a career route without having to take on management responsibilities. Something like 20 per cent of your timetable is 'outreach' work; for example, support of teachers in other schools, helping with the induction and mentoring of newly qualified teachers, participating in initial teacher training. The scheme has been controversial as it has been seen by some as divisive, singling out some teachers and not others. Some schools and some authorities have shied away from it. However, the government is committed to increasing the number of ASTs and maybe as many as 5 per cent of teachers will be ASTs. Again, you have to satisfy standards.

Why would you want to go through this process? The best reason is that you have something to say about teaching and want to disseminate your ideas in school. For example, Karen was a teacher who had done inspiring work with children for whom English was an additional language, and wanted to share her ideas with colleagues, and Jon was a teacher who wanted to develop self-assessment practices in his LEA. A second reason is that being an AST offers a more varied role, combining classroom teaching with support, training and mentoring roles. Third, there is an enhanced AST pay scale (for details go to the DfES web site given in Appendix B). What are the down-sides? First, you might want to put your energy into pursuing a more managerial role and AST might seem a distraction. Second, the proce-dure is draining, inevitably involving the production of a portfolio of evidence and a stressful lesson observation and interview. You might put in a lot of work only to find you have not been awarded AST status. Third, you really need to make sure your colleagues and SMT are supportive of your application. If you are interested in finding out more, the DfES offers a range of advice and guidance services (see glossary in Appendix B), while your LEA will also have a dedicated AST coordinator to arrange outreach work and help in the sharing of ideas and experience.

Relationships with children

Will excess workloads dent your motivation to teach? Chapter 1 suggested that while your interest in your subject was important, as were potential career rewards, it was your relationship with pupils that was central to your decision to teach. The job really is about seeing someone do something with your help which they could not do otherwise. Chapter 2 described how you might well feel particu-larly committed in your first years of teaching. This commitment need not disappear but its focus may change. For example, Sara felt a sense of both gain and loss as she became a more experienced teacher:

> When I first started it was all so special. It's hard to explain but I loved my classes, or at least most of them. I had this tutor group for two years and they were lovely. I missed them so much when they moved on. And I had these exam classes, I took some of them through their GCSE for two years and it meant so much to me when they did well. I don't know if it is because I am older or what but I don't feel the same way. I am so much better at knowing how to help them, I can see what they know, what they don't know and what to say to push them on, but I am not so close to them. It is not the same now. I still enjoy it most of the time but I can see that there was something so special about the way I was learning with them (the pupils) and it will never be like that again.

The sense of detachment is both inevitable, you cannot continue with the same degree of emotional commitment as you started, and valuable, it allows you to more easily reflect on your work as a teacher. In Sara's situation, you might restore the novelty in the job by taking on new roles or undertaking professional development. Recognise that the satisfaction of seeing pupils learn changes but does not go away and even the most experienced teachers continue to feel bound up with pupils' lives. The feedback they get from pupils, parents and other professionals still matters very, very much. And because it matters you will always feel vulnerable as a teacher. In the course of your early career you will have met teachers who have been disillusioned by teaching and regretted their career choice. Many have worked through exceptionally difficult times, they have experienced huge changes in political direction and what has seemed, at times, orchestrated campaigns against teachers and schools in the press. On a personal level they might have lacked support for their career, felt trapped in the wrong school and unable to see a way out. You, too, will have many reasons to become disillusioned – a badly handled incident, being passed over for a promotion, a change of ethos in the school that leaves you high and dry, a comparison with a friend who earns much more than you. My hope is that you enjoy teaching as a career, that you find the right level of challenge and support in your school and that this book has given you an orientation to the pleasures and, perhaps, disappointments that await. The last word goes to Rebecca, now in her third year of teaching:

> I go into work in the morning and I look at other people doing what they are doing and where they are going and I think, 'Yes, I am pleased to be going to school.' Whatever else happens I know it will not be boring, something will happen that will push me, surprise me, make me think about things in a different way. And when schools work well they are such special places. There are children in my class and I think where else in their lives are they going to get someone to care so much for them? It doesn't matter how good or bad they are at something, a teacher will always pick out something they have done well and give them something to go for. There are some hard and diffi-cult pupils and they have got through to me at times, but one of the things you first learn in teaching is that if they really didn't want to be here, there is nothing we could do to stop them. You can see behind the swagger that they care very much. And you can see behind the groaning that we might do afterwards, we care very much too.

Summary

This chapter has looked at:

*   challenge and support in school;
*   moving school;
*   the nature of CPD;
*   thinking outside the box;
*   workloads;
*   the motivation to teach.

A key message is that your career development is greatly affected by the challenge and support in the school in which you are working in.

Appendices

Finding the right school

There is no doubt that finding the right school is the key to developing your career as a teacher. This appendix will help you:

- reflect on what is a suitable school for you;
- make a good impression at interview;
- assess the support you are being offered.

A suitable school

Priorities for most people are to find a school in which they feel they can make a difference, a school in which they feel they will fit, and somewhere in which they can become a better teacher. This means looking for a school in which you feel you would be effective; for some teachers this might mean working in a fairly challenging school in which academic attainment is particularly low, for some a school with particularly strong academic traditions. A suitable school is one in which you feel sympathy with the ethos; for example, you might seek out, or ignore, posts in the independent sector, single-sex schools, middle schools or schools with or without sixth forms. You might be attracted to schools that specialise in working with children with special needs or that have specialist status in the arts, science or technology, or a reputation for liberalism or 'traditional standards'. If you have a family you might look for a post in the school that your children attend or will attend, other people seek at all costs to avoid this. A particular challenge welcomed by some is to work in schools with large numbers of pupils from ethnic minorities.

As a new teacher you are entitled to a programme of support including a reduced timetable, opportunities for observation and feedback on your lessons and a professional mentor, but the spirit in which support is offered is the key. The best way of finding out about support in a school is to organise a visit: most schools would welcome this if you explained that you were interested in applying for a job. Talk to members of the department and find out from new teachers how they have been supported: are they being observed, are they being shown new approaches to teaching and are they getting feedback on their teaching? Some schools, particularly ones linked to a training partnership, might encourage you to get to know the pupils by visiting and working with some classes. Of course, much could change before you take up your post. A particularly valued professional mentor might leave, the school might be faced with a staffing crisis, your head of department might go sick, but schools with a tradition of supporting new teachers are more likely to find ways around this.

It is surprising how often the right choice of school is more a matter of luck than judgement. In many countries there is very little choice in where you end up teaching, teachers are employed by the central or local authority and you will be placed where they think fit. In England and other countries you are, in practice, free to apply to work in the school of your choice and to move schools, as long as you can persuade an interview panel that you are best suited to the job. Nonetheless, the odds are stacked against you in making the best choice. Jobs appear on the market at different times so you might end up accepting a job in, say, March and find a more suitable one advertised in April. You are rarely given much time to think things over and you might be pressurised to 'take it or leave it' on the spot. Psychologically it is very difficult to reject a job after spending the whole day hearing someone extol the virtues of the school. It is not considered acceptable to withdraw from a job you have accepted and this has led to professional difficulties in the past. At a time of teacher shortages this is less likely to be a problem but it is not advisable.

One way you can exert some control over your choice of school is to contact a school in which you would like to work and ask if there are any jobs. This can be surprisingly fruitful if there are teacher shortages. Alternatively, you might like to approach the school in which you are being trained. Indeed, many schools may have entered into a training arrangement because they are looking for someone to fill a post. Of course, this can create a delicate situation if you decide to reject the school or they end up employing someone else, but this discomfort should pass. Whatever your circumstances you have the right to turn down a job if it does not suit you.

Focus questions

- What are your priorities in looking for a school in which to work?
- If you have been offered a post can you see strengths and weaknesses in the programme of support offered to you next year?

Interviews: making an impression on the school

There is a lot of well intentioned and useful advice from employers and institutions on making a good impression on a school. This will stress the importance of a coherent letter of application, your presentation at interview and supporting evidence of your work. You are expected to show eagerness and enthusiasm but not naivety; this is not just at the interview itself but throughout the time you are at school. One school regularly monitored interviewees and their willingness to engage pupils in conversation when being shown around. It is increasingly common for you to be asked to plan and teach a short lesson as part of the interview process. This might seem unfair as you do not know the class but it is a quite understandable procedure. Take it as a sign that the school is taking the recruitment process seriously, and as an opportunity to find out something about the children you want to teach. In a similar vein look positively at those few schools that have experimented with pupil panels as part of the interview process. As for the formal interview itself, there is no certainty about the questions that will be asked but a pooling of experiences among student teachers revealed common themes. First came general questions about your motivation to teach, questions such as: Why do you want to teach? Why teach with your qualifications? What do you get out of teaching? Questions to do with the all-round nature of the job were also common: What can you offer the school in addition to your subject specialism? From your experience what is the most important aspect of pastoral care in the school? Further questions probed your own evaluation of your teaching: What are your strengths as a teacher? What are your weaknesses? Can you tell us about a lesson that was good and why it was good? Can you tell us about a lesson that did not work well and why this was the case? How do you deal with pupils with special needs in your class? How do you deal with gifted and talented pupils? Then, not surprisingly, there were several specific questions about teaching your subject. These naturally differ according to what is most lively and controversial in your subject at the time but examples included: How have you dealt with teaching a specific topic in the school syllabus? What experiences have you had of teaching at key stage 3? What do you feel are the strengths of the new national strategy (or a recent report or new national guidelines) on the teaching of your subject? Can you give examples of how the use of ICT has contributed to the teaching of your subject? Further questioning might probe why you want to work in this particular school especially if there are special features such as single sex, a commitment to mixed-ability teaching or the involvement of the Church.

The answers you give will be strongly tailored to your own particular circumstances but useful advice is to provide whatever you can in the way of examples of your approach or your experience. 'I am interested in using ICT in teaching my subject, for example, I used it to get pupils to design an online newsletter' provides the evidence of your enthusiasm to use ICT especially if you have brought examples of pupils' work along. You will also want to show that you can learn from your experiences; for example, admit a weakness in your teaching is differentiation (we all have difficulty with this) but show you have at least tried to do something about it; for example, you pay close attention to the reading age of materials and try to provide an entry point for all pupils.

One very good piece of advice is to rehearse your answers in your head and then role play an interview with a friend. Some people apply for a post that they do not particularly want in order to get interview practice. This is a question of balancing pros and cons. What you gain in practice is offset by the realisation that you did not perform as well as you could because your heart was not in it.

How a school can impress you

An open school would welcome your interest in an advertised post and suggest you come in to visit. At interview, a school that took your training seriously would be clear about the support it offered you and the arrangements for observation and induction mentor meetings. A senior manager would arrange for you to speak with new teachers and encourage you to ask questions. You would be shown a human face, everyone will recognise the demanding nature of the interview process and teachers will be open about the difficulties and challenges the school faces as well as the successes. You will not be pressurised into accepting the post. A school can best impress you by convincing you that it is providing you with the opportunity to become a better teacher. Once you have accepted a post in school you will want to make sure you visit again before the start of the new term.

For you to do

If you are going for an interview rehearse the interview with a friend. Make sure you have collated examples of pupils' work and other evidence of your teaching such as lesson plans, written feedback from pupils and resources you have prepared. Make a list of questions you want to ask about how the school will support you next year.

Glossary

Note that web addresses were last viewed in May 2005, and may have been altered; however, a simple search will often uncover a new location.

Advanced skills teacher (AST)
An AST is a teacher who has passed a national assessment and been appointed to an AST post. ASTs spend 20 per cent of their time working with teachers from other schools. For more information, go to DfES web site (www.dfes.gov.uk/ast).

A levels
Advanced Level qualifications, more specialist courses typically for post-16 students seeking entrance to higher education. For more information about the qualifications framework, go to the Qualifications and Curriculum Authority (www.qca.org.uk).

Beacon schools
Beacon schools are rated as among the 'best performing' in the country and offer advice on subject teaching, pupil monitoring, school management, provision for gifted and talented children, improving parent involvement, special educational needs and so on. The Beacon school programme is being phased out and schools are encouraged to become involved in the Leading Edge Partnership Programme (www.standards.dfes.gov.uk/beaconschools).

Challenging behaviour
Covers anything from emotional problems through to adolescent attention seeking to outright naughtiness.

Exclusion
Suspension of pupil from school. For more advice on procedures and policies, see DfES Teachernet (www.teachernet.gov.uk/management/workingwithothers/safeschools/exclusion).

Fast track

An opportunity for those seen as highly talented teachers to progress rapidly in their careers. The scheme is usually associated with teacher training programmes but is available once you have started teaching. For more information, go to the Fasttrack web site (www.fasttrackteaching.gov.uk).

General Certificate of Education/GCSE

Academic examination of basic secondary education generally taken by 16-year-olds.

Graduate Teacher Programme

An employment-based teacher training programme.

Head of department (HoD)

Person responsible for the subject curriculum in school, unlikely to be a member of a senior management team.

Independent Schools' Council (ISC)

Represents UK's accredited independent schools. For more information, go to Independent Schools Council information service (www.isis.org.uk).

Induction tutor

Teacher, usually a senior teacher, responsible for induction arrangements in a school.

Key stage

Key stage 3 covers Years 7, 8 and 9, i.e. pupils aged 11–14, key stage 4 covers Years 10 and 11, i.e. pupils aged 14–16.

Learning support assistant (LSA)

An assistant providing classroom support for pupils with special educational needs and/or disabilities.

Local education authority (LEA)

Responsible for educational provision within a local area.

Mentor

Teacher who oversees training and support of new teachers. Many training programmes distinguish between school-based mentors and university-based tutors.

National Literacy Strategy at Key Stage 3

National strategy aiming to improve standards in literacy. For more information, go to DfES standards web site (www.standards.dfes. gov.uk/literacy).

National Strategy at Key Stage 3

The Key Stage 3 National Strategy extended the national literacy and numeracy strategies by offering curriculum guidance and materials for teachers of English, mathematics, science, ICT and foundation subjects (history, geography, technology, modern foreign languages, music, art and religious education and PE). Go to DfES standards site (www.standards.dfes.gov.uk/keystage3).

Newly qualified teacher (NQT)

Recently qualified teacher, i.e. someone in their first year of teaching.

Personal, social and health education (PSHE)

PSHE deals with pupils' health, life skills and citizenship. For more information, go to DfES Teachernet www.teachernet.gov.uk/pshe.

Qualified teacher status (QTS)

Awarded on successful completion of a training programme.

Senior management team (SMT)

This consists of head teacher, deputy head and possibly other senior teachers.

Special educational needs coordinator (SENCO)

Teacher responsible for ensuring that children with learning difficulties and emotional/behavioural problems receive appropriate support and oversees the completion of individual education plans and liaises with external agencies.

Tutor

Someone, usually a lecturer, who oversees training and support of new teachers. Many courses distinguish between school-based mentors and university-based tutors.

Vocational courses

These are designed to prepare students in jobs such as business, construction, engineering, health and social care. They can be taken as part of a package with other qualifications and come in three levels: foundation, intermediate and advanced. For more information about the qualifications framework, go to the Qualifications and Curriculum Authority (www.qca.org.uk).

Appendix C

Organisations mentioned in this book

Note that web addresses were last viewed in May 2005, and may have been altered; however, a simple search will often uncover a new location.

British Council
www.britishcouncil.org
UK's international organisation for educational opportunities and cultural relations, represented in 109 countries worldwide. The British Council oversees training exchange programmes and international collaborative projects via the Central Bureau (www.centralbureau.org.uk).

British Educational Communications and Technology Agency (BECTa)
www.becta.org.uk
BECTa is a government-funded agency that evaluates and supports the use of information and communications technology (ICT). BECTa is responsible for developing the National Grid for Learning (NGfL) and the virtual teachers' centre. The BECTa site provides comprehensive information for all educational levels including lifelong learning, subject-specific advice and general information about using ICT in teaching and learning.

British Educational Research Association (BERA)
www.bera.ac.uk
A membership organisation for those involved and interested in educational research.

Department for Education and Skills (DfES)
www.dfes.gov.uk
Government department responsible for education and training across all sectors of the population in England. The DfES web

site is huge with links to statistics, policy-making documents, circulars and teacher support materials.

DfES's CPD website

www.teachernet.gov.uk/professionaldevelopment

The CPD web site is a one-stop-shop for ideas, examples and opportunities that can support continuing professional development.

European Council of International Schools

www.ecis.org

A membership organisation for international schools. It provides a range of services to its members as well as information about international schools to the general public, and advertises jobs online.

General Teaching Council for England (GTC)

www.gtce.org.uk

Professional body for teaching, which seeks to provide a voice for teachers in government and society at large, concerned with professional development and standards in the profession. The web site has an exceptionally good link to sites of interest. For Scotland, see General Teaching Council for Scotland (www.gtcs. org.uk) and Wales, General Teaching Council for Wales (www. gtcw.org.uk).

National Educational Research Forum (NERF)

www.nerf-uk.org

An independent organisation aiming to raise the quality, profile and impact of educational research. The web site holds the Current Educational Research Database (CERUK) (www.ceruk.ac.uk/ ceruk). See also the Scottish Council for Education Research (www.scre.ac.uk).

National Grid for Learning

vtc.ngfl.gov.uk

Gateway to educational resources on the internet including classroom materials (virtual teachers' centre), resource sharing and discussion. The NGfL portal was launched in November 1998, as part of the government's National Grid for Learning strategy to help learners and educators in the UK benefit from information and communications technology (ICT). It is funded by the Department for Education and Skills and managed by the British Educational Communications and Technology Agency (BECTa).

In Scotland, see the Scottish virtual teachers' centre (www.svtc.org.uk).

Office for Standards in Education (OFSTED)

www.ofsted.gov.uk

Non-ministerial government department responsible for inspection and regulation of education and childcare. Inspections cover schools and colleges, education authorities and initial teacher training courses. It also reports on the impact of government initiatives. Web site carries inspection and other reports.

Qualifications and Curriculum Authority (QCA)

www.qca.org.uk

A non-departmental public body responsible for quality and coherence in the school curriculum, assessment and examinations, and for the framework of general and vocational qualifications.

Scottish Executive Education Department, Scotland

www.scotland.gov.uk

For information on education specific to Scotland.

Standards and Effectiveness Unit

www.standards.dfes.gov.uk

This site is managed by the DfES and provides materials and guidance for creation of schemes of work, literacy and numeracy strategies, education action zones, pupil performance, gender and achievement, parent participation, homework and school improvement. Material on the Key Stage 3 Strategy can be found within the web site (www.standards.dfes.gov.uk/keystage3).

TeacherNet

www.teachernet.gov.uk

Developed by the Department for Education and Skills as a resource to support the education profession, the site contains teaching resources, reports and materials, and opportunities for registering and taking part in online discussion. It is a valuable reference point for any questions you might like to ask about teaching. A section of the site is dedicated to CPD (www.teachernet.gov.uk/professionaldevelopment).

Teacher Training Agency (TTA)

TTA oversees recruitment of new teachers, the quality of initial teacher training and the induction of newly qualified teachers. The corporate web site (www.tta.gov.uk) contains reports and news. The teacher recruitment web site (www.canteach.gov.uk) contains a lot of useful information for people considering entry into teaching, including routes into teaching, training provision, information for newly qualified teachers, and in-service for practising teachers. Publications can generally be downloaded.

Welsh Assembly Education and Lifelong Learning Committee
www.learning.wales.gov.uk
For information on education specific to Wales.

Subject associations and support for teaching

Note that web addresses were last viewed in May 2005, and may have been altered; however, a simple search will often uncover a new location.

Some of the organisations to support you in your subject teaching are listed. Where possible there is a contact for a subject association, followed by two or three sites for curriculum support. Nearly all of these sites will contain links to other sites. Go to the GTC web site (www.gtce.org.uk) for a much longer list of organisations that support teachers and schools or the virtual teacher centre within the National Grid for Learning (vtc.ngfl.gov.uk) for a comprehensive list of sites that support subject teaching.

Art

Access Art
www.accessart.org.uk
Access Art is the web site of the Arts Education Exchange, a non-profit-making organisation, founded in 1999. It is an online visual arts workshop for children and adults, based around artist-led education in museums, galleries and schools.

National Society for Education in Art and Design
www.nsead.org
The society is concerned with art, craft and design across all phases of education in the UK. The web site provides access to a range of resources including publications, a product marketplace, a children's art gallery and information on career opportunities in art and design.

Design and Technology

Barking and Dagenham Bridges Project
> www.bardaglea.org.uk/bridges
> An initiative of Barking and Dagenham Department of Education to examine structures and bridges between cultures.

Design Council Education
> www.designcouncil.org.uk/design
> The Design Council aims 'to inspire the best use of design by the UK, in the world context, to improve prosperity and well-being'. The Education Overview section of the Design Council web site has links, created with partners in education, to a range of learning materials and projects.

National Association of Advisers & Inspectors in Design and Technology
> www.naaidt.org.uk
> NAAIDT has a general aim of support for purposeful practical activity. It coordinates D&T Online (www.dtonline.org) which offers free access to a wide range of design and technology (D&T) materials, resources and software for pupils to use as they engage in design and technology activities as part of the National Curriculum.

Economics and Business

Economics and Business Education Association
> www.ebea.org.uk
> The Economics and Business Education Association represents teachers and lecturers of economics, business studies and related subjects in schools and colleges throughout the UK. The web site has useful links to other sites.

English and Drama

English Resources
> www.englishresources.co.uk
> The site provides free resources for teaching and revising English language and literature.

National Association for the Teaching of English (NATE)
www.nate.org.uk
NATE is the UK subject teacher association for all aspects of English from pre-school to university. The web site contains details of conferences and publications.

Poetry Zone
www.poetryzone.ndirect.co.uk
Poetry Zone is an interactive poetry web site for children and teen-agers to publish their own poetry and reviews. It also contains poems by well-known children's poets and educational material for teachers.

Teachit
www.teachit.co.uk
A teacher-generated site of resources for teachers of English, drama and media studies.

Geography

Field Studies Council
www.field-studies-council.org
An independent educational charity that promotes understanding of the environment.

Geographical Association
www.geography.org.uk
A national membership organisation that provides information and resources to teachers and students of geography and promotes the role of geography in education.

Mapzone
www.mapzone.co.uk
Ordnance Survey's interactive education resource.

History

Cadbury History
www.cadburylearningzone.co.uk/history
The site contains primary evidence sources from the extensive Cadbury archives. Teachers need to register with the site.

Historical Association
www.history.org.uk
The association brings together people who share an interest in the past and in the teaching of history at all levels. The site has details of services, publications, conferences and historical tours.

SchoolHistory.co.uk
www.schoolhistory.co.uk
Resources put together by a practising history teacher.

ICT

Association for ICT in Education
www.acitt.org.uk
The Association for ICT in Education supports the teaching and coordination of information technology in schools. The web site contains downloadable publications and a section with information on events and activities, and discussion groups.

ICT Strand of the Key Stage 3 Strategy
www.standards.dfes.gov.uk/keystage3/strands/?strand=ICT
The ICT strand of the Key Stage 3 Strategy differs from other strands as it contains teaching material, albeit material that will need to be adapted to different contexts.

Mathematics

Association of Teachers of Mathematics
www.atm.org.uk
The Association of Teachers of Mathematics was established to encourage a more learner-centred approach to the teaching of the subject. The web site provides details of courses, conferences and membership information including local branches.

Centre for Innovation in Mathematics Teaching
www.ex.ac.uk/cimt
The centre is a focus for research and curriculum development in mathematics teaching and learning; the web site has access to resources.

Mathematical Association
www.m-a.org.uk
The Mathematical Association aims to bring about improvements in the teaching of mathematics and to provide a means of communication among students and teachers of mathematics. The web site has sections on the teaching of the subject and on association activities.

National Royal Institution Cambridge Homerton
www.nrich.maths.org.uk
NRICH aims to establish a permanent national centre for curriculum enrichment to provide mathematical learning support for

very able children of all ages. The NRICH site is an online maths club with puzzles and problems aimed at very able children.

Modern Foreign Languages

Association for Language Learning (ALL)
www.languagelearn.co.uk
ALL is the major subject association for those involved in teaching modern foreign languages (MFL) at all levels and in all languages. The ALL site provides information on membership, links to language organisations and examination and assessment authorities.

Centre for Information on Language Teaching and Research
www.cilt.org.uk
An independent charitable trust that aims to provide professional support for teachers of languages across all sectors of education in the UK, and to promote a greater national capability in languages.

Music

MusicTeachers.co.uk!
www.MusicTeachers.co.uk
This is a free service that aims to support musicians in every aspect of education and performance. The web site has a useful link to other sites of interest.

SchoolBand
www.musicbyarrangement.co.uk/schoolband
SchoolBand offers help and advice for teachers wanting to start their own orchestra or band.

Physical Education

Duke of Edinburgh's Award
www.theaward.org
A voluntary, non-competitive programme of practical, cultural and adventurous activities, designed to support the personal and social development of young people aged 14–25.

Outward Bound Trust
www.outwardbound-uk.org
A non-profit organisation committed to excellence in outdoor experiential education. It offers challenging adventures year round for adults and youths.

Physical Education Association in the United Kingdom
tele-school.org.uk/pea
The association promotes physical health of the community through physical education, health education and recreation.

Religious Education

Association of RE Inspectors Advisers and Consultants (AREIAC)
www.areiac.org.uk
Professional association for RE inspectors, advisers and consultants. Publishes a range of advice, details of conferences and inset for teachers.

Professional Council for Religious Education (PcfRE)
www.pcfre.org.uk
Subject association for teachers of RE in England, offers support, advice and a forum for exchange.

Science

Association for Science Education (ASE)
www.ase.org.uk
ASE supports science education from primary through to tertiary levels. The ASE site has a teacher zone that includes bulletin boards, discussion groups, teachers' resources, links for science, other education and online media, as well as links to UK and international professional bodies. The site contains SciShop (www.scishop.org), an online resource area for key stage 3 science.

British Gas – Think energy
www.think-energy.com/
This site provides information and advice on the subject of energy and energy efficiency with activities for 11–14-year-olds in the students' zone, as well as classroom resources and forums for teachers.

Science Museum Exhibitions online
www.sciencemuseum.org.uk/on-line
Contains exhibitions about the history of science, scientific people and events and online activities and experiments for children.

Social science

Association for the Teaching of the Social Sciences

www.le.ac.uk/education/centres/ATSS/atss.html

The association aims to encourage and promote the teaching of the social sciences in primary, secondary, further and higher education. The site contains information on events, conferences and membership with useful links to other sites.

Pastoral issues and citizenship

Britkid

www.britkid.org

This is one teacher's guide for young people who do not live or go to school in areas that are ethnically mixed. There is a teacher's guide to help with lesson planning.

Bully Online

www.bullyonline.org/workbully

Bully OnLine is the web site of the UK National Workplace Bullying Advice Line. The web site looks at bullying of adults as well as children at school.

ChildLine UK

www.childline.org.uk

ChildLine is a free, 24-hour helpline for children and young people in danger. The home page for ChildLine has a link for children and young people and one for adults.

Citizenship Foundation

www.citfou.org.uk

The Citizenship Foundation is an independent charity that promotes citizenship education through a wide range of programmes.

National Association for Pastoral Care in Education

www.warwick.ac.uk/wie/napce

For those with an interest in pastoral care and personal–social education. It is a membership organisation.

YourTurn.net

www.yourturn.net

YourTurn.net is part of a campaign to encourage young people to think in new ways about their town or city and their world.

More general curriculum resources

4 Learning

www.4learning.co.uk/secondary

Online resources for teachers, pupils and home learners and a guide to Channel 4's programmes for schools.

BBC Schools Online

www.bbc.co.uk/education/schools

Listings of BBC programmes and resources online for home learning and curriculum. Bitesize (www.bbc.co.uk/schools/revision) is a well-known secondary school resource for examination revision.

Department for Culture, Media and Sport

www.culture.gov.uk

The department is responsible for museums, galleries and libraries, the built heritage, arts, sport, education, broadcasting and the media and tourism, as well as the creative industries, and the National Lottery.

Learning Alive

www.learningalive.co.uk

Resources for schools to communicate, publish their own web pages and find education links run by RM Plc.

Teachers TV

www.teachers.tv

An editorially independent television channel offering support for teachers, the website lists programmes and further online support.

Support for teaching pupils with special needs

Autismconnect

www.autismconnect.org

Autismconnect is a non-commercial web site that aims to be the first port of call for anyone interested in autism.

British Association of Teachers of the Deaf (BATOD)

www.batod.org.uk

BATOD represents the interests of teachers of hearing-impaired children and young people in the UK.

British Dyslexia Association (BDA)

www.bda-dyslexia.org.uk

The BDA provides a forum for the latest thinking and research on dyslexia.

Centre for Special Educational Needs

www.teachernet.gov.uk/wholeschool/sen

Part of the National Grid for Learning, the Centre for Special Educational Needs provides a range of advice and materials for all those interested in, or working with, children with special educational needs.

Centre for Studies on Inclusive Education

inclusion.uwe.ac.uk/csie

CSIE is a British educational charity giving information and advice about inclusive education and related issues.

Dyslexia Institute

www.dyslexia-inst.org.uk

An educational charity for the assessment and teaching of people with dyslexia, and for the training of teachers.

Dyspraxia Foundation

www.dyspraxiafoundation.org.uk

The foundation exists to support individuals and families affected by developmental dyspraxia, and to increase understanding and awareness.

National Association for Gifted Children

www.nagcbritain.org.uk

A membership organisation of parents, teachers and other professionals. It aims to provide help, support and encouragement to gifted children and their families.

National Association for Special Educational Needs (NASEN)

www.nasen.org.uk

NASEN aims to promote the education, training, advancement and development of all those with special educational needs.

National Autistic Society (NAS)

www.nas.org.uk

A leading charity for people with autism and Asperger syndrome.

Royal National Institute for Deaf People

www.rnid.org.uk

A membership charity that aims to achieve a better quality of life for deaf and hard of hearing people.

Royal National Institute for the Blind (RNIB)

www.rnib.org.uk

RNIB offers information, support and advice to the 1.7 million people in the UK with a serious sight problem.

Teacher unions

Association of Teachers and Lecturers (ATL)
www.askatl.org.uk
**National Association of Schoolmasters/
Union of Women Teachers (NASUWT)**
www.nasuwt.org.uk
National Union of Teachers
www.nut.org.uk
Professional Association of Teachers
www.pat.org.uk

Other teacher support

Teacher Support Network
www.teacherline.org.uk
Support and advice service for teachers including free 24-hour telephone and online counselling.

References

(Note that web addresses given were last viewed in May 2005 and may have been altered since then; however, a simple search will often uncover a new location.)

Adams, C. (2003) 'Teacher Retention: facing the challenges', keynote speech at North of England Education Conference, 7 January 2003, GTC, Birmingham.

Allen, P., Warwick, I. and Begum, J. (2004) *New in our Nation*, Lucky Duck Publishing, Bristol (this booklet is also available from the Refugee Council, London).

Banks, F. and Shelton Mayes, A. (eds) (2001) *Early Professional Development for Teachers' Pedagogy*, David Fulton Publishers, London.

Berger, P. and Luckmann, T. (1991) *The Social Construction of Reality: a treatise in the sociology of knowledge*, Penguin, Harmondsworth.

Black, P. and Wiliam, D. (1998) *Inside the Black Box: raising standards through classroom assessment*, King's College, London.

Bleach, K. (2000) *The Newly Qualified Secondary Teacher's Handbook*, David Fulton, London.

Bloom, B.S. (ed.) (1956) *Taxonomy of Educational Objectives: the classification of educational goals: Handbook I, cognitive domain*, Longmans, Green, New York.

Bourne, J. and Blair, M. (1998) *Making the Difference: teaching and learning strategies in successful multi-ethnic schools*, DfES, London.

Brooks, V., Abbott, I. and Bills, L. (2004) *Preparing to Teach in Secondary Schools: a student teacher's guide to professional issues in secondary education*, Open University Press, Berkshire.

Bruner, J. (1996) *The Culture of Education*, Harvard University Press, Massachusetts.

Bubb, S. (2000) *The Effective Induction of Newly Qualified Primary Teachers: an induction tutor's handbook*, David Fulton, London.

Bullough, R., Knowles, G. and Crow, N. (1991) *Emerging as a Teacher*, Routledge, London.

Capel, S., Leask, M. and Turner, T. (2001) *Learning to Teach in the Secondary School: a companion to school experience*, 3rd edn, Routledge, London.

Carnell, E. and Lodge, C. (2000) *Supporting Effective Learning*, Paul Chapman, London.

Chambers, G. and Roper, T. (2000) Why Students Withdraw from Initial Teacher Training, *Journal of Education for Teaching*, 26, 1, 25–43.

Children of the Storm (1998) *Invisible Students: practical and peer-led approaches to enhancing the educational and emotional support for refugee children in schools*, Children of the Storm, London.

Comber, C., Watling, R., Lawson, T. *et al.* (2002) *ImpaCT2 – Learning at Home and School: case studies*, BECTa, Coventry.

Commission for Racial Equality (2000) *Learning for All: standards for racial equality in schools*, CRE, London.

Cowley, S. (2003) *How to Survive Your First Year in Teaching*, Continuum International Publishing Group, London.

De Corte, E., Verschaffel, L., Entwistle, N. and van Merriënboer, J. (eds) (2003) *Powerful Learning Environments: unravelling basic components and dimensions*, Pergamon, Oxford.

Department for Education and Skills (2000) *National Literacy Strategy: supporting pupils learning English as an additional language*, DfES, London, available from the DfES's Standards site at www.standards.dfes.gov.uk/literacy/publications/?pub_id=10009&top_id=0&art_id=0.

Department for Education and Skills (2001) *Key Stage 3 National Strategy: literacy across the curriculum*, DfES, London.

Department for Education and Skills (2002a) *Training Materials for the Foundation Subjects: assessment for learning in everyday lessons*, DfES, London, available at DfES's Key Stage 3 strategy site at www.standards.dfes.gov.uk/keystage3/respub/fs_trmat.

Department for Education and Skills (2002b) *Raising Standards and Tackling Workload – A National Agreement: joint statement from the signatories*, DfES, London, available at DfES's TeacherNet site at www.teachernet.gov.uk/management/remodelling/cuttingburdens/remodeladvice/.

Department for Education and Skills (2003a) *Behaviour and Attendance*, DfES, London, booklets available at DfES's Key Stage 3 strategy site at www.standards.dfes.gov.uk/keystage3/publications/?template=down&pub_id=2481&strand=generic.

Department for Education and Skills (2003b) *Pedagogy and Practice: teaching and learning in secondary schools: Unit 10 group work*, DfES, London.

Department for Education and Skills (2003c) *Teaching and Learning in Secondary Schools: Unit 1 structuring learning*, DfES, London.

Department for Education and Skills (2003d) *Implementing the National Agreement: guidance for schools*, Workforce Agreement Monitoring Group (WAMG), DfES, London.

Desforges, C. (ed.) (1995) *An Introduction to Teaching: psychological perspectives*, Blackwell, Oxford.

Devereux, J. (2001) Pupils' Voices: discerning views on teacher effectiveness, in F. Banks and A. Shelton-Mayes (eds) *Early Professional Development for Teachers*, David Fulton Publishers, London.

Dewey, J. (1997) *How We Think*, Dover Publications, New York.

Dillon, J. and Maguire, M. (eds) (2001) *Becoming a Teacher: issues in secondary teaching*, Open University, Buckingham.

Drever, E. (2003) *Using Semi-Structured Interviews in Small-Scale Research: a teacher's guide*, SCRE Centre, Edinburgh.

Drever, E. and Cope, P. (1999) Students' Use of Theory in an Initial Teacher Education Programme, *Journal of Education for Teaching*, 25, 2, 97–109.

Elliot, D. (1984) My First Year of Teaching, *British Journal of Music Education*, 1, 1, 49–52.

Fullan, M. (2001) *The New Meaning of Educational Change*, Teachers College Press, New York.

Furlong, J. and Maynard, T. (1995) *Mentoring Student Teachers*, Routledge, London.

Gardner, H. (1993) *Multiple Intelligences: the theory in practice*, Basic Books, New York.

Gilbert, F. (2004a) *I'm a Teacher Get Me Out of Here*, Short Books, London.

Gilbert, F. (2004b) You've Got to Show You're God, and Have Proof of It in Your Planner, *Guardian Education*, 20 April 2004.

Gilroy, P. and Wilcox, B. (1997) OFSTED, Criteria and the Nature of Social Understanding: a Wittgensteinian critique of the practice of educational judgement, *British Journal of Educational Studies*, 45, 1, 22–38.

Gold, Y. and Roth, R. (1993) *Teachers Managing Stress*, Falmer, London.

Gorard, S. and Taylor, C. (2003) Editorial – In Praise of Educational Research, *British Educational Research Journal*, 29, 5, 1–4.

Guardian Education (2004) Remodelling, What It Means for Schools, *Guardian Education*, 20 April 2004.

Hallam, S. (2004) *Homework: the evidence*, Institute of Education, London.

Hammond, M. (2002) 'Two Up': a case study exploring new information and communications technology teachers' experiences of their second year of teaching, *Teacher Development*, 6, 2, 225–244.

Hammond, M. (2004) Issues in Using ICT in School, in I. Abbott, E. Bills and V. Brooks (eds) *Preparing to Teach in Secondary Schools*, Open University Press, Berkshire.

Hammond, M. and Cartwright, V. (2003) 'Three Up': a case study of teachers of information and communications technology in their third year of teaching, 7, 2, 211–228.

Hannam, C., Smyth, P. and Stephenson, N. (1976) *The First Year of Teaching*, Penguin, London.

Harrison, C., Comber, C., Fisher, T. *et al.* (2002) *ImpaCT2 – The Impact of Information and Communication Technologies on Pupil Learning and Attainment*, BECTa, Coventry.

Hartas, D. (2004) Special Educational Needs and Inclusive Schooling, in I. Abbott, E. Bills and V. Brooks (eds) *Preparing to Teach*, Open University Press, Berkshire.

Hay McBer (2000) *A Model of Teacher Effectiveness*, DfES, London, available from DfES's TeacherNet site www.teachernet.gov.uk/docbank/index.cfm?id=1487.

Herzberg, F. (1971) Motivation – Hygiene Theory, in D. Pugh (ed.) *Organization Theory*, Penguin, Harmondsworth.

Keys, W. and Fernandes, C. (1993) *What Do Students Think About School? Report for the National Commission on Education*, National Foundation for Educational Research, Berkshire, UK.

Kyriacou, C. (1992) *Essential Teaching Skills*, Nelson Thornes, Gloucester.

Kyriacou, C., Haltgreen, A. and Stephens, P. (1999) Student Teachers' Motivation to Become a Secondary School Teacher in England and Norway, *Teacher Development*, 3, 3, 373–381.

Lave, J. and Wenger, E. (1991) *Situated Learning: legitimate peripheral participation*, Cambridge University Press, Cambridge.

Leach, J. and Moon, B. (eds) (1999) *Learners and Pedagogy*, Paul Chapman Publishing, London.

Lewis, I. and Munn, P. (2004) *So You Want to Do Research? A Guide for Teachers on How to Formulate Research Questions*, SCRE Centre, Edinburgh.

Lortie, D. (1975) *The Schoolteacher: a sociological study*, University of Chicago Press, Chicago.

Marland, M. (2002) *The Craft of the Classroom*, Heinemann, London.

Marland, M. and Rogers, R. (1997) *The Art of the Tutor: developing your role in the secondary school*, David Fulton, London.

Maslow, A. (1970) *Motivation and Personality*, Harper and Row, San Francisco.

McNiff, J., Whitehead, J. and Lomax, P. (1996) *You and Your Action Research Project*, Routledge, London.

Mercer, N. (1995) *The Guided Construction of Knowledge: talk amongst teachers and learners*, Multilingual Matters, Clevedon.

Mercer, N. (2000) *Words and Minds, How We Use Language to Think Together*, Routledge, London.

Moore, W. (2004) *Teachers and Stress: pressures of life at the chalkface*, Channel 4, London, published at www.channel4.com/health/microsites/0-9/4 health/stress/saw_teachers.html.

Munn, P. and Drever, E. (1999) *Using Questionnaires in Small-Scale Research: a teacher's guide*, SCRE Centre, Edinburgh.

Nathan, M. (1995) *The New Teacher's Survival Guide*, Kogan Paul, London.

Oberski, I., Ford, K., Higgins, S. and Fisher, P. (1999) The Importance of Relationships in Teacher Education, *Journal of Education for Teaching*, 25, 2, 135–150.

Office for Standards in Education (1999) *Raising the Attainment of Minority Ethnic Pupils*, OFSTED, London, and available at www.ofsted.gov.uk/publications/index.cfm?fuseaction=pubs.summary&id=771.

Office for Standards in Education (2001) *Managing Support for the Attainment of Pupils from Minority Ethnic Groups*, OFSTED, London, and available at www.ofsted.gov.uk/publications/index.cfm?fuseaction=pubs.summary&id=3441.

Office for Standards in Education (2002) *Achievement of Black Caribbean Pupils: good practice in secondary schools*, HMI 448, OFSTED, London, and available at www.ofsted.gov.uk/publications/index.cfm?fuseaction=pubs. summary&id=63.

Office for Standards in Education (2003) *Quality and Standards in Secondary Initial Teacher Training*, inspected 1999/2002, HMI 546, OSFTED, London, and available at www.ofsted.gov.uk/publications/docs/3308.pdf.

PriceWaterhouse (2001) *Teacher Workload Study Final Report*, DfES, London, and available at www.teachernet.gov.uk/docbank/index.cfm?id=3165.

Reid, I. and Caudwell, J. (1997) Why Did Secondary PGCE Students Choose Teaching as a Career? *Research in Education*, 58, 46–58.

Rogers, B. (1997) *You Know the Fair Rule*, Prentice Hall, London.

Rotter, J. (1989) Internal Versus External Control of Reinforcement: a case history of a variable, *American Psychologist*, 45, 489–493.

Rutter, J. (2001) *Supporting Refugee Children in 21st-century Britain*, Trentham Books, Stoke.

Schön, D. (1987) *Educating the Reflective Practitioner*, Jossey-Bass, San Francisco.

Shaw, B. and Hammond, M. (2003) *A Masters Programme to Support the Early Professional Development of Teachers*, A market research report, University of Warwick, Warwick.

Shulman, L. (1986) Those Who Understand: knowledge growth in teaching, *Educational Researcher*, 15, 4–14.

Simpson, M. and Tuson, J. (2003) *Using Observations in Small-Scale Research: a beginner's guide*, SCRE Centre, Edinburgh.

Smith, A. (1996) *Accelerated Learning in the Classroom*, Network Educational Press, Stafford.

Smithers, A. and Robinson, P. (2003) *Factors Affecting Teachers' Decisions to Leave the Profession*, Brief number 430, DfES, London, and available at dfes.gov.uk/research/data/uploadfiles/RR430.pdf.

Somekh, B. Lewin, C., Mavers, D. *et al.* (2002) *ImpaCT2 – Pupils' and Teachers' Perceptions of ICT in the Home, School and Community*, BECTa, Coventry.

Soulsby, D. and Swain, D. (2003) A Report on the Award Bearing Inset Scheme, DfES, London, available at DfES's TeacherNet site last viewed at www.teachernet.gov.uk/docbank/index.cfm?id=4129.

Spear, M., Gould, K. and Lee, B. (2000) *Who Would be a Teacher? A review of factors motivating and demotivating prospective and practising teachers*, NFER, Berkshire.

Stones, E. and Morris, S. (1989) Pedagogical Studies in the Theory and Practice of Teacher Education, *Oxford Review of Education*, 15, 1, 3–15.

Teacher Training Agency (2003a) *Qualifying to Teach, Professional standards for qualified teacher status and requirements for initial teacher training*, TTA, London, and available at www.tta.gov.uk/php/read.php?sectionid=110& articleid=459.

Teacher Training Agency (2003b) *Results of the Newly Qualified Teachers Survey 2002*, published at the TTA web site, www.tta.gov.uk/php/read.php?sectionid=174

Teacher Training Agency (2003c) *Career Entry and Development Profile*, TTA, London, and available at www.tta.gov.uk/php/read.php?sectionid=191&articleid=1321.

Teacher Training Agency (2003d) *Into Induction: an introduction for trainee teachers to the induction period for newly qualified teachers*, TTA, London.

Thody, A., Gray, B. and Bowden, D. (2000) *The Teacher's Survival Guide*, Continuum, London.

Tomlinson, P. (1995) *Understanding Mentoring: reflective strategies for school-based teacher preparation*, Open University Press, Buckingham.

Tooley, J. (1998) *Educational Research: a critique*, OFSTED, London.

Totterdell, M., Heilbronn, R., Bubb, S. and Jones, C. (2002) *Evaluation of the Effectiveness of the Statutory Arrangements for the Induction of Newly Qualified Teachers*, Institute of Education, University of London, and available at www.teachernet.gov.uk/docbank/index.cfm?id=3100.

Travers, C. and Cooper, C. (1996) *Teachers under Pressure*, Routledge, London.

Turner-Bisset, R. (2001) *Expert Teaching: knowledge and pedagogy to lead the profession*, David Fulton, London.

Wragg, E. (1993) *Class Management*, Routledge, London.

Wragg, E. and Wood, E. (1995) First Encounters with their Classes, in B. Moon and A. Shelton Mayes (eds) *Teaching and Learning in the Secondary School*, Routledge, London.

Index